JN274569

根付●高円宮コレクション II

NETSUKE

The H.I.H. Prince Takamado Collection II

根付について熱心に語られる殿下

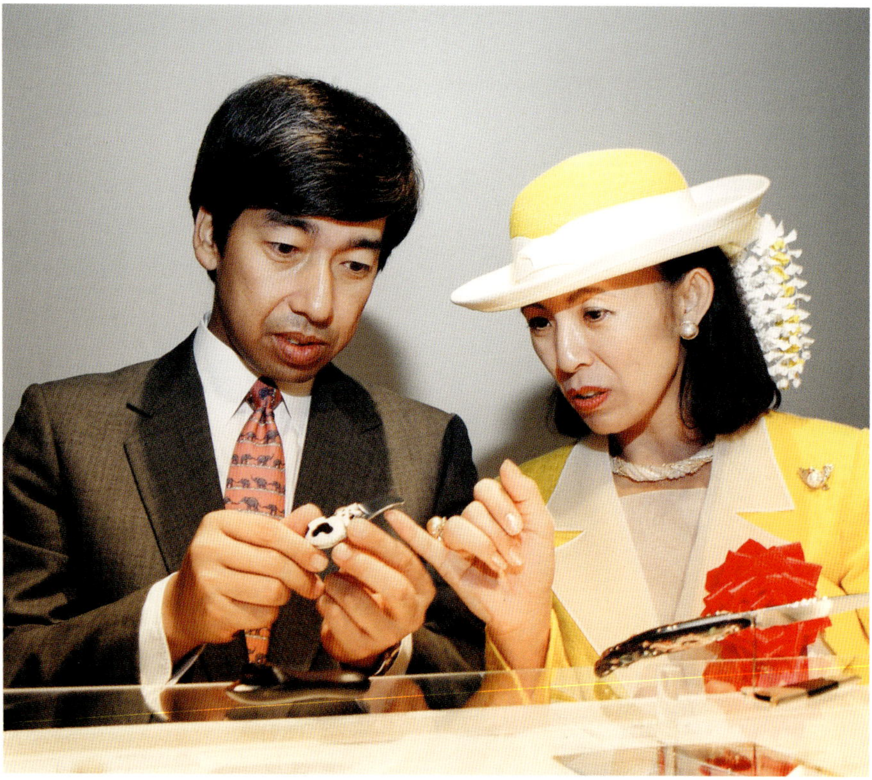

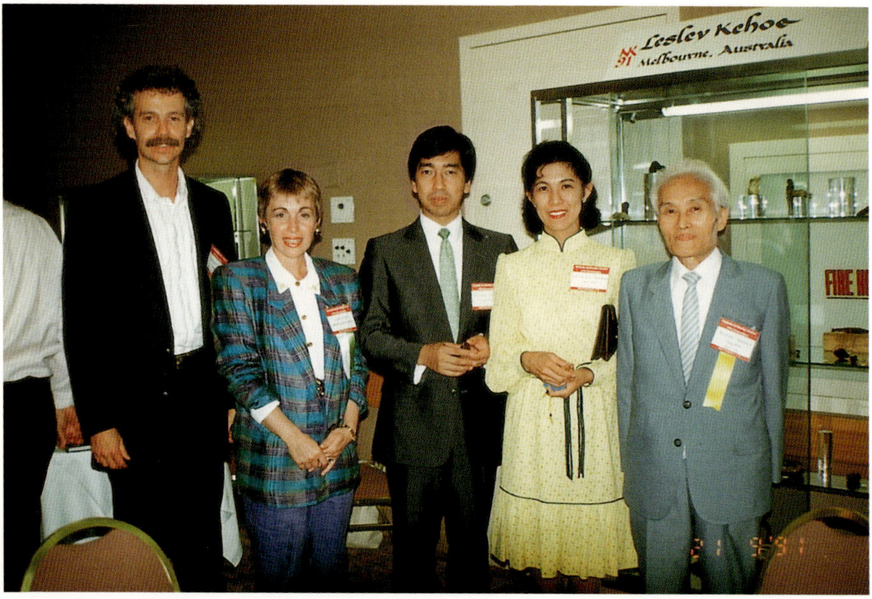
Lesley Kehoe
Melbourne, Australia

序　文

高円宮妃久子

　蒐集家というものは誰しも自分の集めたものに誇りと自信を持っており、その蒐集品が記録に残ることを喜びます。宮様も例外ではいらっしゃらず、いつの日にか、ご自分のコレクションが書物として、より多くの方の目に触れることを密かに願っていらっしゃいましたので、2003年に宮様の現代根付コレクションの本が出版されたとき、私はとても嬉しく思いました。しかし、ページ数の制限や構成上の理由により、ちょうど現代根付の内三分の一ほど、記載することができませんでした。どの根付を載せるかの選択をせまられた時は、選ばれない根付が何とも不憫に思えたのを覚えております。

　このたび、その現代根付の出番がやっと回ってきました。何となく心の中に痞えていたものが一つとれたような気がいたします。又、宮様のお集めになった50点弱の「古根付」ならびに「印籠」「緒締」「小柄」なども掲載する運びとなりました。大変ありがたいことと思っております。

　さて、宮様はよく「根付病に感染してしまった原因は久子にある」と仰っていらっしゃいましたが、確かにその通りで、宮様にお目にかかる以前から、私は根付を集めておりました。その後、宮様がお集めになったものとは比べ物になりませんが、英国に滞在中、大英博物館とヴィクトリア＆アルバート博物館で根付を見たのをきっかけに、少しずつ自分のお小遣いで買える範囲内で集め始めておりました。気に入ったものと買えるものが一致せず、よく彫られているのに、たった一ヶ所の破損がゆえに、コレクターが眼もくれないようなものを譲ってもらったこともあります。

　私にとってはどれも大事な根付でしたので、いつも身近に飾っており、それが宮様のお目にとまって、興味をおもちになりました。これが宮様の根付病の始まりです。その後におもとめになった最初の根付、「十二神将

の午」を私の誕生日のプレゼントとしてくださいました。婚約発表のちょうど２週間くらい前のことです。

　夫婦揃って共通の趣味があり、好みも似ているということはとても幸せなことです。縁あって出会えた作品の数々をお手に取り、ゆっくりご覧になるお姿はいつもとても穏やかでした。新しい根付をお持ち帰りになると片手で包み込むようになさって、そっと私の差し出す手の中に入れてくださいました。私の反応をじっとご覧になるのも楽しみの一つにしていらしたように思います。

　読者の皆様にはこのコレクションを通して宮様のそのようなお人柄に少しでも触れていただければこの上ない喜びでございます。

　最後にこの本の出版にあたり多くの方のお世話になりました。ご尽力いただいた関係者みなさまに心より御礼を申し上げます。

平成18年１月

PREFACE

H.I.H. Princess Hisako Takamado

I believe it is inherent in every collector to feel a sense of pride in his collection and to revel in having it on record. My late husband was no exception. He secretly hoped that one day he would be able to publish a book about his netsuke collection and thereby be able to share these cherished pieces with a greater audience. When this dream became a reality in 2003, the year after his passing, with the publication of a book entitled "Contemporary Netsuke: The H.I.H. Prince Takamado Collection," I was truly delighted for him. However, due to considerations of design and space, about one third of the netsuke could not be included, and I had to make quite a few heart-rending decisions.

Now it is the turn of these pieces to come into their own, and I must confess I feel a sense of relief. The responsibility of choosing certain netsuke as opposed to others, and wondering if my husband's choices would have been the same, weighed heavily upon me. This book includes all the contemporary netsuke that we did not include in the first book, his antique netsuke collection (which, though quite small, is the result of many years of careful selection) and also the *inro, ojime* and *kozuka* that he accumulated on the way.

My husband often said that he caught the netsuke disease from his wife. I suppose that I have no choice but to say that that is an accurate account of what happened. As a university student, I came across netsuke for the first time at the British Museum and the Victoria and Albert Museum, and was fascinated. In my own way and within the confines of my own pocket money (suffice it to say that it was a small pocket!), I was the owner of a little netsuke collection. Often, I suffered from the mismatch between what I liked and what I could afford; sometimes, I took home a beautifully carved, but chipped, piece that most collectors would by-pass! Of course, it was nothing like the sophisticated collection put together by His Highness, but I was still proud of the pieces that I had acquired.

Wherever I lived, I would display the netsuke so that my guests could touch them. And so it happened that they caught the eye of the then young prince. He was very interested in them, and when he bought his first netsuke, "Twelve Guardian Deities - Horse" by Kenji, he gave it to me as a birthday present. This was just a fortnight before the official announcement of our engagement.

It is a wonderful thing for a husband and wife to share an interest. I often watched His Highness pick up and look at his netsuke, and he always looked to be so much at peace. Whenever he brought a new netsuke home, he would ask me to put my hands out, he would put the piece in my hands and close my fingers around it. Then he would watch my face to see my reaction as I opened up my hands and studied the new addition to our collection. It became a little ritual that we both enjoyed.

Through this book, I hope that the readers will be able to feel His Highness's warm personality, his sense of humor, and his ever-encouraging presence.

I would like to take this opportunity to express my appreciation to all those who were involved in the production of this book. My thanks go to all of them.

January 2006

根付蒐集の喜び

高円宮憲仁親王

　私が根付を集めるようになって八年ほどになる。妻がもともと学生時代から集めていたものだが、根付を扱う店に連れていってもらってからは私がすっかり虜になってしまった。妻は英国に長く住んでいたので根付を見る機会が多く、日本に帰る度に少しずつ買っていたようだ。私の方は根付が現在も作られているなど思いもかけなかったので、実物を見てその意匠の面白さ、可愛さ、彫刻技術の素晴らしさに驚いてしまった。あんまり驚いたので、婚約のプレゼントというか、妻への最初のプレゼントは根付になった。これが私の買った根付第一号である。

　印籠や煙草入れなどの提げ物を提げる時に、その紐の端に結び付けて帯から落ちないようにする道具が「根付」である。その名称の由来については、そもそもは木の根っこを使っていたからという説と、紐の根元に付けるからという説とがある。このような用途のものははるか昔より存在していたわけだが、「根付」の語が初めて記録に登場するのは、寛文11年（1671）刊の『賓臓』という書物が最初であるらしい。
　江戸中期には一般に喫煙が大流行し、これが全国的に根付が普及する大きな原因の一つになったようだ。皆が煙草入れを携帯するようになり、根付が必需品になったわけである。絵師、仏師、鍔職人、蒔絵師、面師、欄間師、金工職人などの専門職人が副業として盛んに根付を製作するようになり、その中から次第に専門の根付師たちが育っていった。そして文化、文政（19世紀前半）に根付はその最盛期を迎える。象牙、猪牙、鹿角、黄楊、黒檀、琥珀、珊瑚、金属、漆、陶磁器、ガラスなどさまざまな素材を用い、蒔絵や象嵌などの技法も駆使されるようになった。しかし開国後の幕末から明治にかけて日本人が洋服を着るようになると、用途を失った根

付の需要は急速に減衰してしまう。

　ところが、それと同時に日本にやって来た欧米人がこれに大層興味を示し、根付は海外で大変な人気を得るようになり、今度は輸出用にどんどん作られるようになった。しかし大量の注文に応じるにはどうしても質より量を求めるようになる。一部の職人気質の根付師たちを除いて、全般に技術的・芸術的レベルが低下していったのも事実であった。同時に江戸時代から明治にかけての名品のほとんどが海外へ流出してしまったのである。根付の辿った運命は、そういった意味で浮世絵のそれに似ている。しかしそれゆえ、国内需要の少なさにも関わらず根付芸術は生き延びた。第二次大戦後は主に米国のコレクターや業者の応援を得て根付製作の伝統は保たれ、今に至ったのである。現在では6〜70名の根付作家が一所懸命に伝統の芸術を伝えている。

　根付はその形状によっていくつかの名前がつけられている。人物や動物などをその形に彫った形彫根付、円盤型の饅頭根付、それに精緻な透かし彫りを加えた柳左根付、円盤に金属などの蓋をつけた鏡蓋根付、帯の間に挟むように長く作られた差根付などである。根付はその精緻な彫刻技術もさることながら題材が実に豊富であり、滑稽なもの、洒落たものも多い。印籠は武士が使うものだから、美しい蒔絵や象嵌を施して最初から美術品的性格を求めたものだが、根付は一般町人も皆使ったわけで、もっとくだけて面白いものが数多くあるわけだろう。印籠が能なら、根付は狂言であるといえよう。

　根付を説明するのに「ひねり」という言葉を私はよく使う。根付と小彫刻との違いの一番のポイントがそこにある。根付は装身具であるため、どの角度から見てもちゃんと仕事がなされていないといけない。置物の場合は例えば底面は平らで何も彫ってなくとも良いわけだが、根付はそうはいかない。だから逆にそれを生かして、着用している時には見えない側に工

夫を凝らした、あるいは洒落を加えたものが沢山ある。例えば人が床を磨いている図がある。これをひっくり返してみると床が心という字になっている。つまり"心を磨く人"というわけである。編笠を裏返すと中に鬼が潜んでいる。節分の豆まきから隠れているわけだ。編笠の上にはご丁寧にも豆がのっていたりする。

源氏物語や平家物語、三国志などから題材をとった、物語性のある根付も沢山ある。私の所蔵の一つに「サルカニ合戦」という題のものがあるが、これは怪我をして包帯を巻いたカニに頬っぺたを摘まれて痛みに顔をしかめているサルの根付である。もう一方の頬は蜂に刺されて丸く腫れ上がり、またサルの頭を上から眺めるとヘタがついていて柿の実になっている。サルカニ合戦の四つの登場人物（？）を一つの根付に上手くまとめた傑作だと思っている。

提げ物は、例えば印籠、印籠の蓋が着用時に開かないようにするための緒締め、根付の3点で一組になるわけだが、これらを共通あるいは関連した題材で作るような"遊び"も多かった。米俵の印籠に鼠の根付が付いていたり、見ザル・言わザル・聞かザルで3点セットになっているものなどを見たことがあるが、必ずしもコレクターがセットで欲しがらないこと、また業者にとってもバラで売った方が利益が大きいことから、現在セットで残っているものは案外多くないようだ。

集め方にも楽しみがある。冒頭に書いた私の根付第一号は、仏法の守護神である十二神将の午であった。これは私の干支なのだが、その後最初の子供が生まれた時に作者に頼んで妻と子の干支で神将を彫ってもらった。以後、子供が生まれる度に新しく製作してもらい、現在では五人の神将がいるが、これはまだこれからも増える予定である。

根付は実用品だから丈夫にできていなければいけない。角や突出した部分があると欠けたり折れたりしてしまうから、できるだけ丸く滑らかにすることが大切である。重すぎて困るから、結局は掌に収まるくらいで丸っ

こいものが良いということになる。本来であれば部分的に飛び出たり、長く伸びたりする題材や構図であっても、根付である以上それをうまく丸くまとめなければならない。武士の姿を彫る時には刀がどうしても突き出してしまうが、それをいかに身体に沿わせるか、あるいはいっそのこと刀を曲げてしまうか。そしてそれが全く不自然に見えないようにするのが、根付師の腕前である。

　掌で包んだ時の感触というのが実は根付にとって最も大事なことで、いかに見かけが良く出来ていても、握り心地が悪いものは根付としての価値は低い。この掌の感触には作家も大変気を使っており、製作過程でも幾度となく握って掌の感触を確認しながら先へ進んでいく。古今の根付は象牙と黄楊が圧倒的に多い。彫刻素材として優れているのは言うまでもないが、象牙は石と違って温かく、適度な湿り気と重量感があるし、黄楊は特有の温かさと優しさを備えているからだろう。

　芸術品、美術品に対して一番失礼なことは、大切にするあまりしまい込んで死蔵することだと私は思っているので、わが家では根付はすべて応接間や廊下の棚に飾ってあり、時々行って触ってあげることにしている。お客様に根付をお見せする時にも、必ず見るだけではなく触っていただいて、その良さを実感していただいている。そうして愛された根付はだんだん手の脂分によって磨きがかかり、少しずつ摩耗してますます丸く滑らかになりながら「慣れ」と呼ばれる味わいをそなえるようになってくる。象牙は色も変化していく。ちょうど何十年も使われた良い銀製ライターなどの、角が削れて年代物の風格が出てくるのと同じである。

　ワシントン条約の関係で2年ほど前から象牙の輸出入が禁止された。当然根付にとって大打撃になると誰しもが思った。転職せざるを得ない作家が沢山出るだろうし、根付の伝統そのものが消滅してしまうと予想した人もいたかも知れない。しかしこの一大騒動は、予想とは少しばかり違った結果を生み出した。

　まず当然考えられたのは、象牙に代わる新しい素材の開拓だった。マン

モスの牙がシベリアやアラスカから輸入されるようになった。象牙より幾分黄色味を帯びているが、良質のものはあまり象牙とかわらないので立派な代替品となった。河馬の歯は大きさは象牙やマンモス牙に遙かに及ばないが大変に硬く、磨き込むと青白く透明度のある光沢が得られ、なかなか良い素材であることがわかった。何より、河馬の歯は切ってやらないと伸び過ぎて口が閉まらなくなってしまうので、動物園でも時々切ってやっているとのこと。動物を殺したりしないどころか、河馬にとっても結構な話である。米国の業者などの協力で、今まで使われなかった海外の木材も運び込まれた。マホガニー、スネークウッド、ブライヤー（パイプに使われるツツジ科植物の根）などが利用されている。そして今までは象牙しか彫らなかった作家も、他の素材に挑戦するようになった。

　これらの挑戦は新素材に合った技術の会得につながり、それは同時に大きな自信につながった。更に良かったことは、様々な素材を使うことになったお陰で、素材に応じて彫刻技術と題材とを選択するという、非常に基本的なことを作家たちが再発見したことである。象牙は高級品イメージがあって売れやすいから、たとえ木の方が題材や表現方法に適しているところでも、安易に象牙を選んでしまうことが多々あったと思う。根付の一番の重要性が"素材"ではなく"題材"にあること、従ってどんな素材でも根付を作ることができることを再認識する恰好の機会となったのである。根付の将来を考える時、この意味するところは決して小さくない。そして新聞や雑誌のワシントン条約関連の報道が根付も取り上げてくれたことにより、国内での認識が少し高まったことも思わぬ収穫であった。

　根付は今や世界的芸術である。各国にコレクターがいるだけでなく、外国人作家もだいぶ増えてきた。1991年9月にサンフランシスコで開催された根付研究会大会には、米国、カナダ、英国、オーストラリア、ニュージーランド、イスラエル、ジンバブエからの出品があった。しかも技術、意匠ともに素晴らしい作品を作る人が何人も出てきている。何より発想が新鮮である。大会に出席した日本の作家たちへの良い刺激にもなったと思

う。

　根付は、切り取りから仕上げまで一人の手作業で行われるから集中力と時間を要する。それに同じものでなく新しいものを次々に創り出していくわけだから、常に新しいイマジネーションを要求されるので、作家がどんなに頑張っても一ヵ月に一個半から二個というのが限界である。それ以上作ろうとすれば質の低下は避けられない。もし彫っていって木の節やひびが現れてしまったら、たとえ完成目前であってもあきらめるより仕様がない、また一からやり直しである。根付400年の伝統を守って、毎日こつこつと作業を進める作家たちの仕事が、一人でも多くの人に喜ばれるようになってもらいたい。

　日本独自の文化、芸術として発展し、世界中で高い評価を与えられている根付が、その発祥の地で満足な理解を得られていないのは誠に残念なことである。この芸術がわが国でもっともっと愛されるようになって欲しいと願っているのは私一人ではないと思う。

　　　　　　　　　　　　　（初出——講談社『本』1992年1月号）

The Joy of Collecting Netsuke

H.I.H. Prince Norihito Takamado

About eight years have already passed since I began collecting netsuke. My wife had been collecting them since her university days, and after she took me to a shop that sold them I became completely addicted. As my wife had lived in Great Britain for a long time, she had had many opportunities to see netsuke there, and she gradually began buying them every time she returned to Japan. As for me, I could not even imagine that netsuke were still being carved today; so much so that when I actually saw some contemporary netsuke I was astonished at their interesting designs, tenderness, and the great skill with which they were carved. In fact, I was so impressed that the first gift I ever gave to my wife, a kind of engagement present, was a netsuke. That was the very the first netsuke that I ever bought.

When suspending such *sagemono* as *inro* or tobacco pouches, it was a netsuke that people tied to the other end of the string, which they slipped under their *obi* sash, as a toggle to prevent the item from falling. Concerning the origin of the name, there are two explanations: one is that wooden roots (*ne*) were attached (*tsukeru*), and the other is that it was to the end (*ne*) of the string that the toggle was attached (*tsukeru*). There had been items used in such a way since ancient times, but the first recorded use of the name "netsuke" appears in a 1671 publication entitled *Storehouse of Treasures*.

In the mid-Edo period (eighteenth century), the smoking of tobacco became all the rage, and this was a major reason for the spread of netsuke throughout the whole country. Everyone started carrying tobacco pouches, which made it necessary to use netsuke. A number of specialized artisans, such as painters, sculptors, sword-fitting makers, lacquer artists, mask carvers, decorative-railing carvers, and goldsmiths also began to create netsuke, and from among these, artists who specialized in the carving of netsuke arose. Then, during the early nineteenth century (the Bunka and Bunsei eras), the art of netsuke carving entered its golden age. Netsuke were made from a wide variety of materials, including ivory, boar tusk, stag antler, boxwood, ebony, amber, coral, metals, lacquer, porcelain, and glass, and they were often decorated with lacquer *maki-e* techniques or the inlay of other materials. But after Japan opened its doors to the West in the mid-nineteenth century, the Japanese began to wear Western attire, and the demand for netsuke, which were no longer needed, suddenly plummeted and the art form almost disappeared.

However, at the same time, the Westerners who came to Japan were fascinated by netsuke, which thus became so popular abroad that they began to be produced for export. But because the artisans could not make them quickly enough to satisfy the great demand, quantity was given precedence over quality. With the exception of a few netsuke carvers who took pride in their work, the level of technique and the artistic quality reached a nadir. Simultaneously, from the end of the Edo period to the beginning of the Meiji era (mid-nineteenth century), almost all works by master carvers were exported. Thus, the fate of netsuke was very similar to that of *ukiyo-e* woodblock prints. For that reason, even though the domestic demand was very small, the art and techniques of netsuke carving were given a new impetus. After the Second World War, it was mostly due to the support of American collectors and dealers that the art of netsuke carving was preserved and continues to thrive today. At present, there are between sixty and seventy netsuke carvers [in Japan] who are exerting every effort to pass on the traditions of their art.

There are various types of netsuke, and they are classified according to their shape. There are *katabori* ("in-the-round") netsuke that depict human figures and animals; *manju* (discus-shaped) netsuke, among which are works with intricate openwork called *ryusa* netsuke, and others fitted with a round metal lid that are known as *kagami-buta* netsuke; and *sashi* netsuke, which are thrust under the *obi* sash. In addition to netsuke that are characterized by extremely detailed carving techniques, there was a rich catalogue of subjects, and humorous and witty pieces abounded.

Inro were worn by members of the warrior class, and the type of pieces on demand by them were beautiful works of art lavishly decorated with *maki-e* and inlay techniques. But netsuke were also worn by the tradesmen, which is why a great number of interesting, more casual pieces were carved. If *inro* were to be compared with the classical Noh drama, then netsuke would be the equivalent of the Kyogen farces.

When describing netsuke, I often use the word "twist," wherein lies the difference between a netsuke and a miniature carving. Because netsuke are decorative accessories, they had to be carved on all sides, so that they would look beautiful from any angle. In ordinary carvings (*okimono*), for example, the bottom was flattened and left uncarved, but in netsuke that was not done. On the contrary, such areas were often intricately worked, even portions of the piece that were not visible when it was worn; thus, a number of works were imbued with a playful spirit. For example, one popular design shows a man polishing a floor, but when you turn the piece over, what was the floor is revealed as the Japanese character *kokoro*, meaning "heart" or "spirit." Thus, the work depicts "a man refining his heart." In another design, a woven-bamboo hat reveals a demon hiding within it. This work depicts the Bean-Throwing Festival (*Setsubun*), when demons are dispelled by having beans thrown at them—which is why the demon is hiding. Usually the artist was careful to carve a bean or two resting upon the hat.

Subjects were often taken from such classics as *The Tale of Genji*, *The Tales of the Heike*, and *The Romance of the Three Kingdoms*, so netsuke that portray narratives are numerous. Within my collection, there is a work entitled *The Battle between the Monkey and the Crab* (depicting the children's tale of a monkey who steals a crab's persimmons and how the crab gets revenge). This netsuke depicts the face of a monkey that is in severe pain because an injured and bandaged crab is firmly pinching one of his cheeks, and a bee is stinging the other, which is puffed up and swollen. In addition, when you look at the monkey's head from above, the netsuke suddenly becomes a persimmon. I feel that this netsuke is a masterpiece that skillfully portrays all four elements (the monkey, crab, persimmon, and bee) of this popular tale.

Concerning *sagemono*, as an example, *inro* were often worn in a three-piece ensemble of netsuke, *ojime* (the bead that keeps the *inro* closed), and *inro*, and quite often the three pieces were skillfully created so that they were thematically related in terms of subject; for example, a rice-bale *inro* worn with a rat netsuke, or a three-piece set based on the three "Hear no evil, Speak no evil, See no evil" monkeys. But because collectors did not always desire such matching sets, and because dealers sometimes sold them separately in order to make more profit, there are surprisingly few intact sets of matching pieces that remain together today.

There is also much joy to be obtained in collecting netsuke. The first netsuke in my collection, which I mentioned earlier, is a horse; it is actually a horse-headed celestial general, one of the twelve Buddhist guardians. [I had bought this piece because] I was born in the Year of the Horse, and when my first child was born, I asked the same carver to create a piece depicting the guardian deities ruling the years in which my wife and daughter were born. I did this for all of my children, so now I have guardian-netsuke for all five of us, and I hope to increase that number.

As netsuke are items for practical use, they must be durable. Corners and portions that jut out or protrude tend to become damaged or to break off, so it is important to make the piece as round and as smooth as possible. It would cause problems if it is too heavy, so the ideal for a netsuke is that it be round and able to be easily held in your closed hand. Even if the subject or design includes elements that extend far beyond the main body of the piece, to create a good netsuke, those elements must be adroitly deformed and rounded. When carving the figure of a warrior, it is inevitable that his sword would normally stick out, so it is the task of the carver to treat it adeptly, either by having it adhere closely to the body or by "bending" the sword to follow the round contours of the work. It is up to the skill of the netsuke carver to make such "deformed" elements appear perfectly natural.

A very important factor in judging a netsuke is how it feels when held in the palm of the hand, for no matter how brilliantly it is carved, if it does not feel "right" when held, it will not be highly valued as a netsuke. The carvers take great pains in order to achieve the right feeling when held, and they will often, even in the midst of carving a piece, hold it to see how it feels before proceeding further. In netsuke, both antique and modern, those made of ivory and boxwood clearly represent the majority. These materials were very well suited to being carved—ivory is much warmer than stone, has a moderate smoothness, and is relatively heavy; and boxwood has an especially warm quality.

I believe that one of the worst things that one can do with works of art is to treasure them too much and to store them safely away; therefore, in my home, my netsuke are displayed on shelves in the sitting room or in the corridors, and from time to time I pick one up and hold it. And when I show netsuke to guests, I not only have them look at the pieces, but also encourage them to pick them up and hold them, so that they might feel the excellence of the work directly. In this way, my favorite netsuke become polished with the natural oil on my hands, which gradually enhances the feeling of smoothness and roundness, achieving a state that is called *nare* ("broken in") in Japanese. In the case of ivory, the color gradually changes, and just like a good, decades-old silver lighter, the corners become worn down and the work takes on a time-worn quality.

Due to the terms of the Washington Convention, all trade in ivory was banned about two years ago (1989). This was of course seen by everyone as a great blow to the art of netsuke. There were several carvers who were forced to change their careers, and many thought that the art of netsuke might be lost forever. Yet all the great fuss resulted in an unanticipated effect.

Needless to say, everyone first thought of finding another material to substitute for ivory. Then, fossil mammoth tusks began to be exported from Siberia and Alaska. Although mammoth tusk has a slightly yellower cast than ivory, good pieces are practically identical with ivory, so it became a wonderful alternative material. Hippopotamus tooth cannot compare with elephant or mammoth tusks in size, but as it is extremely hard and displays a bluish-white, translucent sheen when polished, it was seen as another excellent substitute. Indeed, because hippo teeth must be cut lest they grow too long, making it impossible for the animals to close their mouths, zoos regularly cut the teeth of animals in captivity. Thus, hippo teeth have the added advantage of being easy to obtain without causing the death of, or even any harm to, the animals. Through the cooperation of American dealers, several foreign materials that had never been used in netsuke carving began to be employed, including ebony (African blackwood), snakewood, and briar (the root of an azalea-related plant, which is used in making pipes). Thus, even artists who had never carved anything but ivory took up the challenge of working with new and different materials.

Concurrent with the challenge of using the new materials, carvers had to develop new techniques that matched the qualities of each material, and this served to boost the morale of the carvers. Moreover, one benefit was that through using several different materials, carvers began to choose subjects and to acquire carving techniques to match the materials, leading them to rediscover anew the very basics of their art. Because ivory was considered a material of very high quality and works made of it were easy to sell, even many netsuke that because of subject matter or mode of expression were better carved out of wood had been made of ivory. But for netsuke, it is not "material" that is important but the "subject." Therefore, the ban on ivory gave the carvers an excellent opportunity to reconfirm that they were able to create netsuke out of almost any material they wanted to use. When considering the future of the art of netsuke, the significance of this is very great. Further, because netsuke were featured in newspaper and magazine articles related to the Washington Convention, another unexpected result was that the Japanese public was made more aware of the art of netsuke.

Today, the carving of netsuke is an international art. Not only are there collectors in several countries; additionally, the number of foreign carvers has increased. At the biennial convention of the International Netsuke Society held in San Francisco (Sept. 1991), there were works on show by carvers from such countries as the U.S., Canada, the U.K., Australia, New Zealand, Israel, and Zimbabwe, and a number of those carvers produced superb works of outstanding craftsmanship and design. More than anything, they partook of a freshness in concept. I think that this provided a great stimulus to the carvers who had attended the convention from Japan.

Because netsuke are completely made by one person—from the cutting of the raw material to the final finishing—their production requires a great deal of concentration and time. And because carvers do not produce the same piece over and over but continuously strive to create new and different pieces, they are constantly in need of new inspiration and flights of imagination. But no matter how diligently they work, carvers are usually limited to producing one or two pieces per month. If they try to carve any more than that, the quality will suffer. And if during the process of making a piece a knot or crack appears in the wood, even in the very final stages of finishing, the carver has no choice but to abandon the work and to start all over from the very beginning. Since the art of netsuke has thrived for four centuries, and the carvers painstakingly pursue their craft incessantly, I would be very pleased if even one more person found joy in the art.

That netsuke, which developed out of the culture and artistic traditions unique to Japan, and which have come to be highly valued around the world, are not fully understood and appreciated in the land of their birth is truly regrettable. I am certain that I am not the only one who hopes that this art will come to be loved more and more within Japan.

—from *Books* (Jan.), Tokyo: Kodansha, 1992

NETSUKE

The H.I.H. Prince Takamado Collection II

目次

序文　　高円宮妃久子	5
根付蒐集の喜び　　高円宮憲仁親王	9
古根付	23
現代根付（日本人作家）	69
現代根付（外国人作家）	159
印籠	171
印籠（現代）	185
緒締（日本人作家）	189
緒締（外国人作家）	201
作品リスト	205
凡例	206
作家略歴	223

CONTENTS

Preface　　H.I.H. Princess Hisako Takamado	5
The Joy of Collecting Netsuke 　　H.I.H. Prince Norihito Takamado	9
Antique Netsuke	23
Contemporary Netsuke (Japanese Artists)	69
Contemporary Netsuke (Western Artists)	159
Inro (Antique)	171
Inro (Contemporary)	185
Ojime (Japanese Artists)	189
Ojime (Western Artists)	201
List of Works	205
Notes	206
Artists' Profiles	223

古根付
ANTIQUE NETSUKE

動　物　ANIMALS

OOI

虎 / Tiger Licking Its Paw
象牙 / ivory
岡佳 / Okatori
2.9cm

後ろ足をなめる虎は丸みを帯びて使い勝手の良い構図。当時、本物の虎を見る機会はなく、中国の絵などを参考に彫った。

This tiger is a well-rounded, easy-to-use work of clever design. There were no tigers in Japan, so artists probably referred to Chinese paintings in order to portray them.

○○2

虎／Tiger
海象牙／marine ivory
無銘／**Unsigned**
2.5cm
長く愛用された跡の慣れが手に取ったときに心地よい。
The *nare* of this obviously long-cherished work makes it feel good in the hand.

ANIMALS　動物—25

003

親子虎 / Tigress with Cub
黃楊 / boxwood
岷江　花押 / Minko, with *kao*
3.9cm

子虎を見つめる母虎のしぐさがとてもやさしい。
The expression of the mother tigress as she looks upon her cub is filled with tenderness.

004

親子牛／Cow with Calf
象牙／ivory
友忠／Tomotada
5.1cm

牛を彫るのを得意とした友忠の小ぶりで愛らしい作品。

Tomotoda was renowned for his carvings of oxen even during his lifetime. This charming netsuke is a relatively small example of his work.

005

猪／Boar
木／wood
光正　花押／Mitsumasa, with *kao*
3.5cm
旧 M. ハインドソンコレクション／ex. M. Hindson Collection
旧 B. ヘップワースコレクション／ex. Barbara Hepworth Collection
旧 M. エデコレクション／ex. Michel Edde Collection
旧 J. カースティンコレクション／ex. Joseph Kurstin Collection

006
　　釣瓶に蛙／Frog on Bucket
　　黄楊／boxwood
　　正直（伊勢）／Masanao (Ise)
　　3.6cm

007
　　石臼に蛙／Frog on Millstone
　　黄楊／boxwood
　　正直（伊勢）／Masanao (Ise)
　　2.7cm

008

鶉／Quail
胡桃／walnut
左一山／Hidari Issan
4.2cm

自然の素材を活かしながら、細かいところまで丁寧に仕上げてある。
The artist made good use of the natural material in this finely detailed carving.

009
鳩／Pigeon
一位／yew
亮芳／Sukeyoshi
3.6cm

010

干鮭／Dried Salmon
鯨鬚／baleen
花押(銕哉)／Tessai (*kao*)
4.1cm
鱗や歯が写実に徹して丹念に彫りこんである。
The scales and teeth are all consistently carved in great detail.

SUPERNATURAL CREATURES　霊獣霊鳥・架空動物

011

親子獅子／Shishi with Young
黄楊／boxwood
正義／Masayoshi
4cm

012

玉獅子／Shishi Holding a Ball
黒檀／ebony
正義／Masayoshi
2.7cm

013
獅子／Shishi
木／wood
友親／Tomochika
4.1cm

014

猩々／Shojo
象牙象嵌／ivory with inlays
光雲／Koun
4.7cm

猩々は中国の想像上の怪獣で人に似ていて、毛は赤くて長く、子どものような声をし、人語がわかり、酒を好んで飲むという。

A *shojo* was an imaginary creature in Chinese mythology that resembled a human. It had long red hair and a childlike face, understood human speech, and loved to drink rice wine!

015

鬼の念仏 / Oni no Nenbutsu
木，珊瑚 / wood, coral
東谷 及び 銀落款(楳立) / Tokoku, with silver seal 'Bairyu'
3cm

016

胡瓜に河童 / Kappa in Cucumber
木，翡翠 / wood, jade
東谷 / Tokoku
4.2cm
旧 M. エデコレクション / ex. Michel Edde Collection
旧 J. カースティンコレクション / ex. Joseph Kurstin Collection

胡瓜を好む河童が胡瓜の中に入っている。
A *kappa*, which loves to eat cucumbers, is here depicted within one.

LEGENDS AND OLD TALES 故事伝説・昔話

017

蘭亭 / 'Rantei' Chinese Palace
黒檀 / ebony
宝楽 / Horaku
4.2cm

353年(永和9年)3月3日、王羲之がこの蘭亭において、当時の名士四十一人と祓禊、曲水流觴の宴を開いた。よく見ると大勢の人の姿が彫ってある。

On March 3, 353, the famous calligrapher Wang Hsi-chih invited some 41 literati to Lanting (Jpn. Rantei). They observed rites of purification and then composed poems as they partook of drinking from little wine cups floated on a winding stream. Inside the building the artist has carved the figures of over thirty people.

不老長寿の桃の中に、西の仙境である崑崙山の女神西王母の姿がある、からくり根付。

This netsuke opens up to reveal the figure of Seiobo (The Queen Mother of the West), who was thought to live on the edge of Paradise just west of the Kunlun Mountains; she is here depicted within one of her fabled peaches of long life and immortality.

018
西王母／**Seiobo Inside a Peach**
鉄刀木，象牙／ironwood, ivory
景利／**Kagetoshi**
3.2cm
旧今井健三コレクション／ex. Kenzo Imai Collection

人生に迷い旅に出た盧生という青年の話。宿屋で悟りがひらけるという枕で寝ると自分が王となり50年、豪華な生活をする夢を見る。目が覚め、人生は所詮、一睡の夢であると悟る。

This is the tale of a youth named Lu Sheng, who had become disillusioned with life. When he naps in an inn on a pillow said to grant enlightenment, he sees a dream in which he is a king who lives in luxury for fifty years. When he awakes, and learns that he had slept for but an instant, he realizes that life is nothing but a fleeting dream.

019
盧生の夢／**The Dream of Lu Sheng**
紫檀／rosewood
景利／**Kagetoshi**
3.2cm
旧 B. ジャースコレクション／ex. Betty Jahss Collection

020
鍾馗と鬼(施灸図)／Shoki and Oni
木／wood
壽玉／Jugyoku
5cm

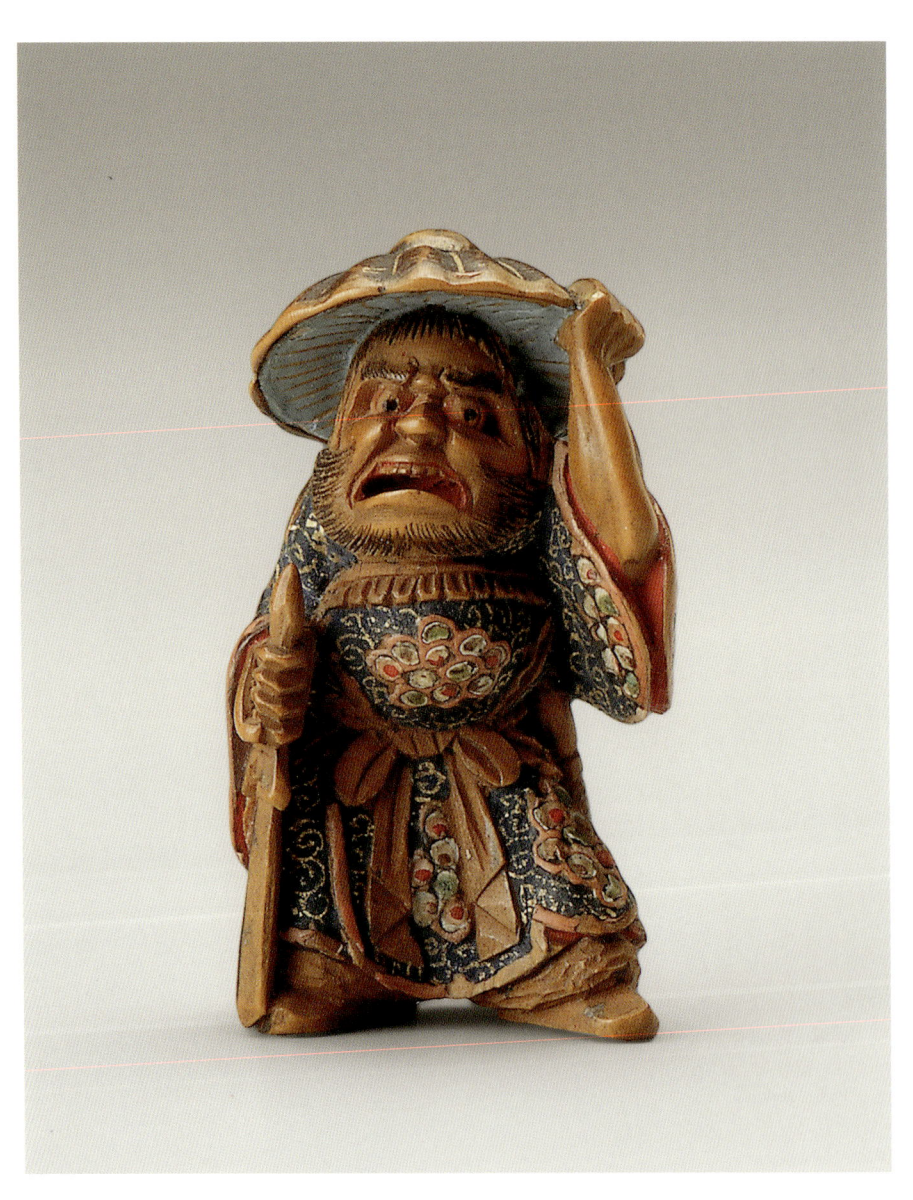

021
鍾馗／Shoki
木刻彩色／painted wood
周山／Shuzan
4.5cm

022

達磨／Daruma with Hossu
木，象牙／wood, ivory
東谷／Tokoku
3.3cm

023
達磨／Daruma with Hossu
木刻象嵌／wood with inlays
光珉／Komin
2.7cm

024
法螺貝に弁慶と烏天狗／Benkei with a Karasu-Tengu
黄楊／boxwood
無銘／Unsigned
6.5cm

025

関羽と魯粛／Kuan Yu and Lu Su

木／wood

萬寿　三月吉日　他／signed Manju, an auspicious day in March
3.6cm

関羽と魯粛は『三国志』に登場する二人の英雄。
Kuan Yu and Lu Su were two heroes of the ancient Chinese classic known as the *Romance of the Three Kingdoms*.

026
三番叟／Sambaso Dancer
黄楊，象牙／boxwood, ivory
法實／Hojitsu
3.9cm
旧 S. コーミーコレクション／ex. Stephen Comee Collection

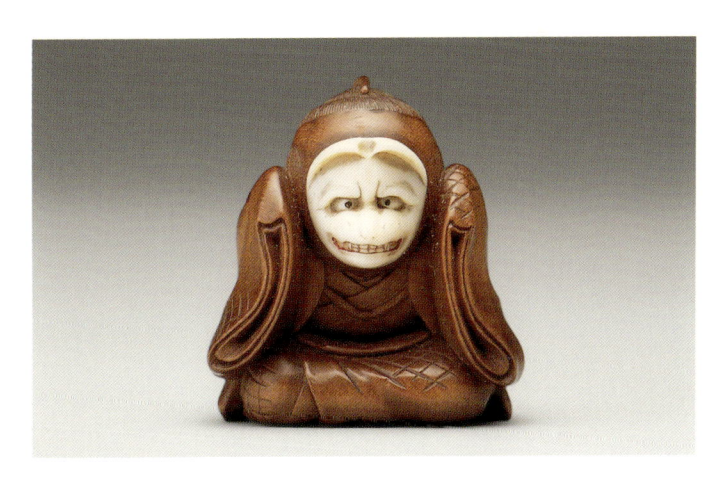

027
面遊び／Boy with Fox Mask
木，象牙／wood, ivory
法實／Hojitsu
3.2cm
旧 M. エデコレクション／ex. Michel Edde Collection
旧 J. カースティンコレクション／ex. Joseph Kurstin Collection

028

大黒に唐子 ／ Daikoku and Karako
象牙 ／ ivory
長雲斎 及び 落款（秀親） ／ Chounsai, with seal 'Hidechika'
3.5cm

029
布袋に唐子 ／ Hotei with Karako
木，象牙 ／ wood, ivory
東谷 ／ Tokoku
4cm
旧 S. メレデスコレクション ／ ex. S. Meredith Collection

030
月に兎／**Lunar Hare**
象牙／ivory
重正／**Shigemasa**
3.5cm
旧 T. ハーンコレクション／ex. Teddy Hahn Collection

031
白蔵主／Hakuzosu (Fox-Priest)
木刻彩色／painted wood
周山／Shuzan
5.4cm

032

葛の葉／Kuzu no Ha
木／wood
正一／Masakazu
3.8cm
旧 M. エデコレクション／ex. Michel Edde Collection

竹田出雲の浄瑠璃『芦屋道満大内鏡』(1734)より童子丸を抱く狐の葛の葉。この子が、陰陽師として知られるのちの阿部晴明である。

Abe no Yasunari saved a young vixen who repays his kindness by taking human form and bearing him a son. This child grew up to be the famous astrologer-statesman, or *onmyoji*, Abe no Seimei.

033
酔いどれ狸／Drunken Badger
木／wood
北哉／Hokusai
2.7cm

LEGENDS AND OLD TALES 故事伝説・昔話

034

孟宗／Meng Tsung in a Bamboo Shoot
木／wood
正次／Masatsugu
5.4cm

筍の中に鍬を持った人が彫ってある。孟宗は中国に伝わる親孝行の話の主人公。病気の老母のために雪深い竹林の中に入り、筍を探した。

An old Chinese story about filial piety. Meng Tsung went into the bamboo forest in winter to search for bamboo shoots for his aged and ailing mother. His figure can be seen carved in minute detail inside the bamboo shoot.

HUMAN FIGURES 人 物

035
蹴鞠人物／Kemari Players
象牙／ivory
無銘／Unsigned
3.8cm
旧ガボール・ウィルヘルムコレクション／ex. Gabor Wilhelm Collection

036
茶人／**Tea Master**
茶木刻彩色／painted tea-plant wood
落款銘／**Signed**
3.8cm

037
茶筅売／Tea-whisk Vendor
木，象牙／wood, ivory
粛斎／Shukusai
4cm
旧 C. モンジーノコレクション／ex. Carlo Monzino Collection

038

宇治人形／Tea-leaf Picker (Uji doll)
共箱　表：御吉例　茶の木　宇治人形　蓋裏：大日本莵道二代楽之軒／
tomobako signed Dai-Nippon Uji Rakushiken II※
茶木彩色／painted tea-plant wood
落款（楽之軒）／Rakushiken (Seal)
3.4cm
旧松林豊斎コレクション／ex. Hosai Matsubayashi Collection
※上林楽之軒の呼称は「らくのけん」として上林家には伝承されている。
　Within the artist's family, the name is read "Rakunoken" Kanbayashi.

039
宇治人形―雨中／Tea-leaf Picker with Raincoat (Uji doll)
共箱　表：御吉例　茶の木　宇治人形　蓋裏：大日本二代楽之軒蒐道／
tomobako signed Dai-Nippon Rakushiken II, Uji
茶木彩色／painted tea-plant wood
落款（楽之軒）／Rakushiken (Seal)
3.4cm
旧松林豊斎コレクション／ex. Hosai Matsubayashi Collection

040

立雛／Tachibina Doll
木刻彩色／painted wood
落款銘／Signed
5.2cm

OTHERS その他

041
波図色絵瓢箪／Gourd
磁器，銀／porcelain, silver
無銘／Unsigned
5cm

042
炭点前／Charcoal basket
木／wood
玉山／Gyokuzan
3.1cm

MASK NETSUKE 面根付

043
能面「黒髭」／Noh mask "Kurohige"
木／wood
天下一　出目左満／Tenkaichi, Deme Saman
4.3cm

MASK NETSUKE　面根付―61

鏡蓋根付 KAGAMIBUTA NETSUKE

044

重陽菊水図／Chrysanthemums
金属，鹿角／metal, stag anther
落款有／Signed
4.0cm

045
楽茶碗／Bottom of Raku Tea Bowl
鉄，鉄刀木，漆／iron, ironwood, lacquer
夏雄（刻銘）・不可花押（金漆）／Natsuo, with *kao* in gold lacquer
3.8cm

046
雉鳴桜花図／Pheasant and Cherry Blossoms
金銀色絵，象牙／metal, ivory
無銘／Unsigned
4.6cm

MANJU NETSUKE 饅頭根付

047
唐子に蓑亀(変わり饅頭根付)／Karako with Tortoise
象牙，蒔絵／ivory, *maki-e*
民谷／Minkoku
3.8cm

緒　締 OJIME

048
蝶に唐子／Karako with Butterfly
象牙／ivory
無銘（民谷）／Unsigned (Minkoku)
1.3cm

KOZUKA 小柄

051
四君子／Four Noble Plants
黒檀／ebony
懐玉斎／Kaigyokusai
9.7cm

表／Front　裏／Back

四君子は蘭(春)、竹(夏)、菊(秋)、梅(冬)の草木。中国宋代よりその気品の高い美しさが図柄や模様に用いられる。また、これら四つの草木を描くにあたって基本的な筆遣いをすべて学ぶるとされ、画法を学ぶ重要な素材となっている。

The Four Noble Plants are the orchid (spring), bamboo (summer), chrysanthemum (autumn), and plum blossom (winter). They were often employed from the Sung dynasty as beautiful patterns expressing nobility and high virtue. They were also treasured among schools of ink painting, because it was said that one could master all techniques simply by studying the basic methods of painting these four plants.

049
龍／Dragon
黒檀／ebony
岷江惇徳　花押／Minko Juntoku, with *kao*
9.8cm

050
龍／Dragon
象牙／ivory
懐玉 及び 落款〈正次〉／Kaigyoku, with seal 'Masatsugu'
9cm

現代根付（日本人作家）
CONTEMPORARY NETSUKE (Japanese Artists)

明　美 AKEMI

OOI

枯／Fallen Leaf
黄楊／boxwood
4.5cm

BISHU 美　洲

002
九尾之狐／Nine-tailed Fox
象牙／ivory
4.0cm

003
峯上／At the Summit
象牙／ivory
4.5cm

004
獲物／Game
象牙／ivory
4.8cm

005
玉兎／Jewel Rabbit
象牙／ivory
3.5cm

71

006
日本之形　虎／Tiger
マホガニー／mahogany
6.8cm

007
鼠，〔緒締〕ねずみ／Rat, 〔*ojime*〕Rat
黒檀，〔緒締〕マホガニー／ebony, 〔*ojime*〕mahogany
3.5／3.1cm

008
猪，〔緒締〕猪／Wild Boar, 〔*ojime*〕Wild Boar
マホガニー，〔緒締〕黒檀／mahogany, 〔*ojime*〕ebony
5.4／3.2cm

GAHO 雅峯

009
ごっつぁんです，〔緒締〕米俵，塩籠／Sumo Wrestler, [*ojime*] Rice Bale, Salt Basket
河馬歯，〔緒締〕河馬歯／hippopotamus tooth, [*ojime*] hippopotamus tooth
5.6cm

010
猛暑／Dog Days
象牙／ivory
4.2cm

悟 堂 GODO

011
蛙の口ジャンケン／Games Frogs Play
象牙／ivory
2.7cm

蛙が口と目でジャンケンをしている。
Frogs playing a game of stone, paper, scissors with their mouths and eyes.

012
我が年／My Year
象牙／ivory
3.2cm

GYOKUSHO 玉 昇

013
猿／Monkey and Young
象牙／ivory
4.2cm

014
碁打ち／Go Player
象牙／ivory
3.1cm

治 彦　HARUHIKO

015
無題／Untitled
石，18金，ルビー／stone, 18K gold, ruby
L 3.7cm

仏さまのご慈悲のなかで、石ころも貴重な宝石も同じ価値。
In the eyes of the Buddha, a common stone and a precious jewel are of the same importance.

016
無題（Ⅱ）／Untitled
瑪瑙，18金／agate, 18K gold
3.4cm

HIDEFUMI 英　文

017
どんこ／**Donko-Fish**
黄楊／boxwood
6.0cm

芳　堂 HODO

018
きのこ狩り／Mushroom Hunt
鹿角／stag antler
5.2cm

HOSEN　宝　泉

019
しめじ茸／Shimeji Mushrooms
象牙／ivory
3.3cm

020
春の七草，〔緒締〕土鍋／
Seven Spring Herbs, 〔ojime〕 Earthenware Pot
象牙，〔緒締〕象牙／ivory, 〔ojime〕 ivory
4.3cm／1.9cm

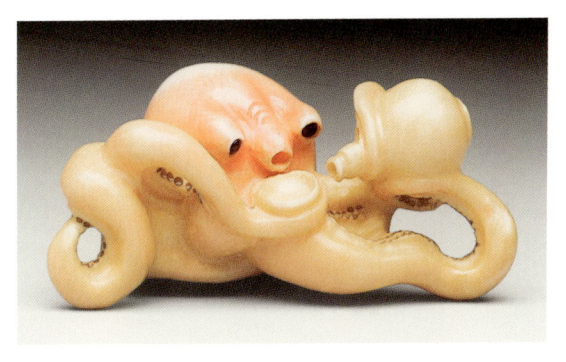

022
蛸／Octopus
象牙／ivory
5.1cm
酒を飲んで顔の赤くなった蛸。
A drunken, red-faced octopus.

021
達磨大師／Daruma
象牙／ivory
4.1cm

79

芳朱 HOSHU

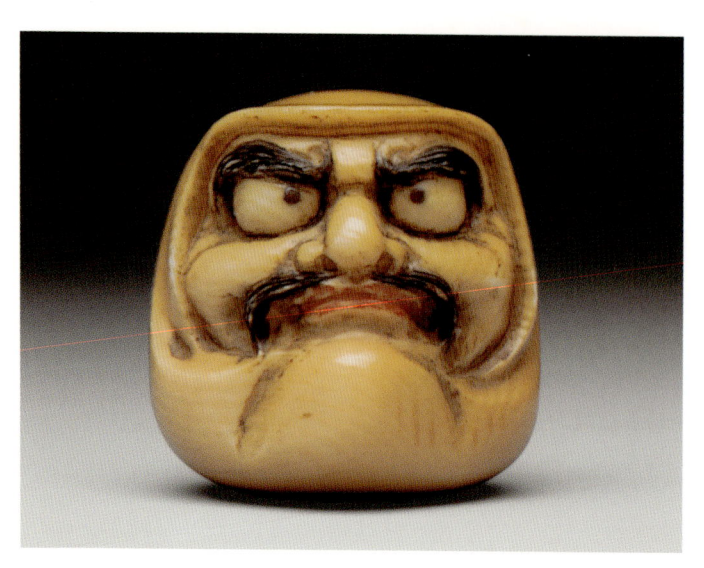

023
達磨/Daruma
象牙/ivory
2.5cm

024
達磨/Daruma
象牙/ivory
2.1cm

ICHIO 一 桜

025
姫だるま／Hime-Daruma
象牙／ivory
4.8cm

一 空 IKKU

026
月うさぎ / **Moon Rabbit**
象牙，鼈甲 / ivory, tortoiseshell
2.7cm

とても小さい根付なのに月の中の兎が丸く彫れている。
A very small netsuke with a full, well-rounded rabbit in the moon.

027
こうもり / **Bat**
マホガニー / mahogany
5.3cm

ISOJI 五十治

028

桜花／Cherry Blossoms
象牙，金蒔絵／ivory, gold *maki-e*
4.1cm

一 舟 ISSHU

029
羽衣／**Hagoromo**
象牙／ivory
5.5cm

能楽師や能面を細密に彫るこの作家の技法をよく表した作品。
A good example of the technique of this artist in carving finely detailed Noh actors and masks.

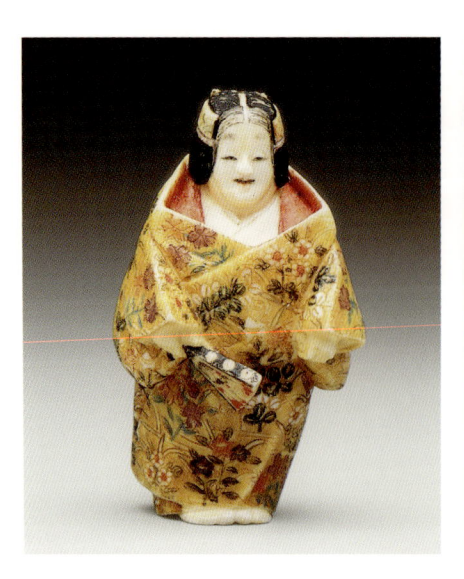

030
熊野／**Yuya**
象牙／ivory
5.1cm

031
面尽くし／**Noh Masks**
象牙／ivory
5.2cm

JIN 仁

032
新巻鮭／Salted Salmon
象牙／ivory
5.0cm

033
早春／Early Spring
象牙／ivory
6.3cm

034
栗／Chestnut
象牙／ivory
3.8cm

035
干しやまめ／Dried Trout
象牙／ivory
10.5cm

寿　光　JUKO

036
海豚／Dolphin
象牙／ivory
2.4cm

037
太古の夢／Ancient Dreams
象牙／ivory
4.5cm

JUSHO 樹　生

038
   菩薩面／Bodhisattva
   象牙／ivory
   3.8cm

039
   裸婦／Nude
   象牙／ivory
   6.0cm

寛玉 KANGYOKU

040
安心して／Relax
象牙／ivory
5.1cm

041
どおり外のことも有るネ！／
Strange Things Do Happen!
ヘラ鹿角／moose antler
3.3cm

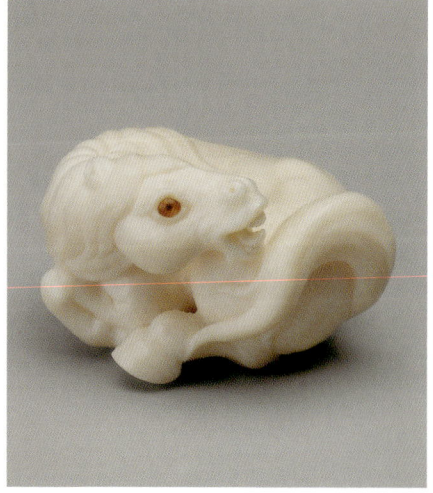

042
いななく／Neighing Horse
象牙／ivory
2.6cm

043
たねうま／Seed Horse
タグアナッツ，鼈甲／tagua nut, tortoiseshell
4.0cm

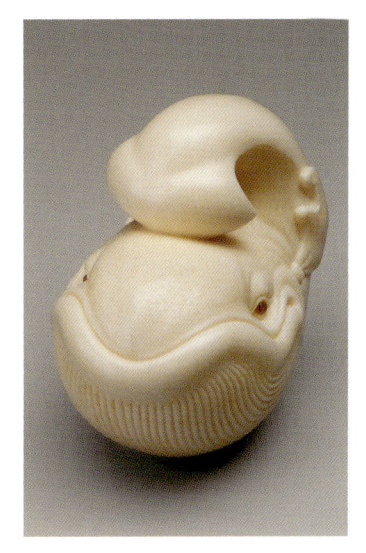

044
鯨／Whale
象牙／ivory
4.8cm

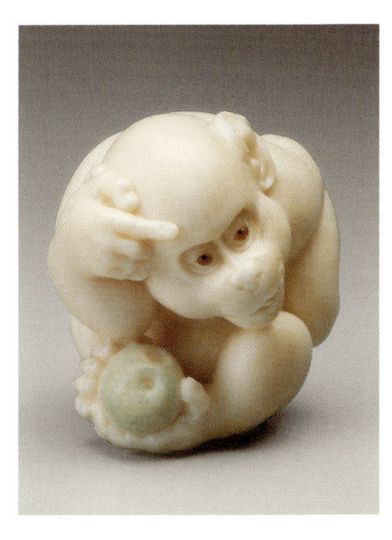

045
見えるの つぎの世紀／
Seeing the 21st Century
象牙／ivory
4.2cm

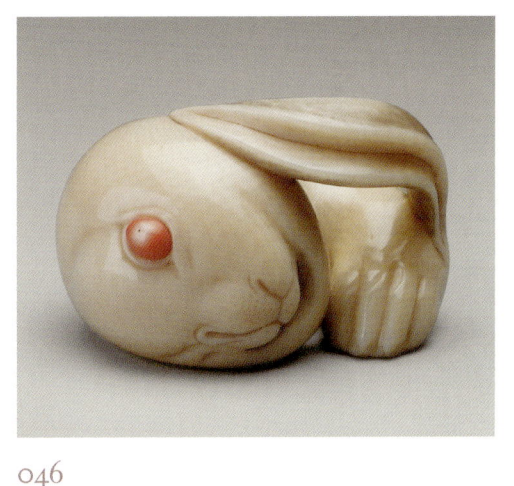

046
幻兎／Surrealistic Rabbit
象牙／ivory
4.1cm
旧キンゼイコレクション／ex. Kinsey Collection

寛　弘 KANKO

047
犬／Dog
象牙／ivory
2.9cm

048
子犬／Puppy
象牙／ivory
2.9cm

KANSUI　寛　水

049
猿／Monkey
象牙／ivory
4.3cm

050
子しし／Baby Shishi
マホガニー，アクリル／mahogany, acrylic
4.0cm

051
午／Horse
象牙／ivory
4.6cm

一 夫 KAZUO

052
碁盤に煙草入れ／Go-Board with Pipe Case
象牙，黄楊，海松／ivory, boxwood, black coral
3.5cm

KENJI 賢次

O53
親子／**Mother and Child**
象牙，紫檀／ivory, rosewood
4.5cm

O54
河童／**Kappa**
象牙，鼈甲／ivory, tortoiseshell
4.1cm

O55
亥／**Boar**
象牙／ivory
3.9cm

056

鶏，〔緒締〕鶏／Rooster, 〔*ojime*〕Hen
琥珀，〔緒締〕琥珀／amber, 〔*ojime*〕amber
4.7cm／2.1cm

057

莢豌豆／Bean Pod
象牙／ivory
5.3cm

KIHO　喜　峰

058
かちかち山／Kachi-Kachi Yama
黄楊，銀，銅／boxwood, silver, copper
4.5cm

059
草薙の剣／Kusanagi no Tsurugi
檜／Japanese cypress
4.8cm
伊勢神宮御遷宮のあと、古いお社の木材で作ったもの。
Made of wood from the old building of the Grand Shrine of Ise after its move.

060
とおせんぼ／You're in My Way
タグアナッツ，金／tagua nut, gold
3.8cm

061
遠い日の夢／Dreams of Long Ago
黒檀，水晶，金／ebony, crystal, gold
5.7cm

062
おにぎり，〔緒締〕柿／Rice-Ball, 〔*ojime*〕Persimmon
マンモス牙，銅，〔緒締〕銅，銀／mammoth tusk, copper, 〔*ojime*〕copper, silver
3.8／1.5cm

063
かいこ／Silkworm
象牙，黒檀／ivory, ebony
8.0cm

064
宇宙観／Universe
マカデミアナッツ，銀／macadamia nut, silver
3.0cm

065
阿吽／Beginning and End
琥珀，象牙，銀／amber, ivory, silver
4.6cm

066
火の鳥／Firebird
琥珀，金／amber, gold
3.7cm

97

067
チェシャーネコ / **Cheshire Cat**
象牙，琥珀 / ivory, amber
3.7cm

『不思議の国のアリス』に登場するチェシャーネコ。ニヤニヤしている口だけ最後まで残して姿を消していく所。

The Cheshire Cat (*Alice in Wonderland*) starting to disappear, leaving just his grin.

068
不思議の国 / **Wonderland**
黄楊，琥珀，銀 / boxwood, amber, silver
4.4cm

こちらのチェシャーネコは上のねじを回すと体が消えていく。

Here the body of the Cheshire Cat disappears when the screw at the top is turned.

069
創世の時 / **The Beginning of Time**
黒檀，金 / ebony, gold
3.6cm

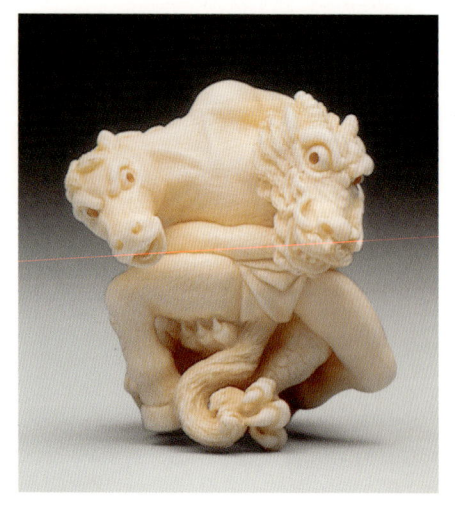

070
名勝負 / **Good Match**
象牙 / ivory
3.1cm

「薬売りの老人が店じまいをするとそこに掛けてある壺に入る。それを見た役人が頼んで一緒に入ると中に立派な御殿があり、そこで飲んで食べて楽しんだ。」という後漢書の故事。

An old Chinese story (from the *Hou Han Shu*). An old man selling medicine folds up his stall at the end of the day and goes into a pot that is hanging there. A famous official sees this and asks to join him. When he gets inside, there is a splendid palace and a lavish banquet. He partakes of this feast before returning to his normal world.

071
壺中天有 / **The Paradise Within**
琥珀，銅，銀 / amber, copper, silver
3.6cm

072
悟空 / **The Monkey King**
黄楊，金 / boxwood, gold
3.8cm

073
つくも / **Tsukumo (*yokai* spirit)**
鹿角 / stag antler
5.1cm

074
毛づくろい / **Grooming**
象牙，プラチナ，金 / ivory, platinum, gold
4.0cm

075
一人旅 / **Lone Journey**
象牙 / ivory
3.6cm

076
金烏玉兎 / **Golden Crow, Silver Rabbit**
琥珀，銀 / amber, silver
3.3cm

中国では太陽に三本足の鳥が、日本では月に兎がいると言われる。殿下を名誉総裁にもつ日本サッカー協会のシンボルが三足烏（八咫烏）であるのに因んで、太陽がサッカーボールの形になっている。

The Chinese say that there is a three-legged bird in the sun: the Japanese say that there is a rabbit in the moon. The sun is carved like a soccer ball in honour of His Highness, who was the honorary president of the Japan Football Association. The JFA has as its emblem a three-legged crow.

KINSUI 欽 水

077
御頭／Lion-Dance Head
黄楊／boxwood
2.9cm

078
花茄子／Eggplants with Frog
黄楊／boxwood
4.4cm

絹 代 KINUYO

079
地球儀，〔緒締〕地球儀／Globe,〔ojime〕Globe
蝶貝螺鈿，金蒔絵，〔緒締〕蝶貝螺鈿，金蒔絵／
mother-of-pearl, gold *maki-e*,〔*ojime*〕mother-of-pearl, gold *maki-e*
3.0cm／2.0cm

080
メロン／Melon
黄楊，蒔絵／boxwood, *maki-e*
3.5cm

081
手鞠／Silk Ball
黄楊，蒔絵／boxwood, *maki-e*
3.4cm

082
あっち行け／Go Away!
タグアナッツ，蒔絵／tagua nut, *maki-e*
4.3cm

083
花手まり / Flower Ball
黄楊,蒔絵 / boxwood, maki-e
3.4cm

084
空の散歩,〔緒締〕太陽 /
Sky Promenade, 〔*ojime*〕Sun
琥珀,漆,〔緒締〕象牙,漆 /
amber, lacquer, 〔*ojime*〕ivory, lacquer
4.0cm / 1.5cm

かわいい風神、雷神そして私が書いた絵本「夢の国のちびっこバク」の主役「バックン」が気球に乗っている。
Promenading through the sky is a little Wind God, a little Thunder God, and the baby Baku from the picture book written by Her Highness, *Katie and the Dream-Eater.*

085
鳳凰 / Phoenix
琥珀,蒔絵,貝 / amber, *maki-e*, shell
4.3cm

086
秋草 / Autumn Flowers
ガラス,蒔絵 / glass, *maki-e*
3.9cm

103

恒 山 KOZAN

087
オーロラ／Aurora
マンモス牙，海松／mammoth tusk, black coral
5.2cm

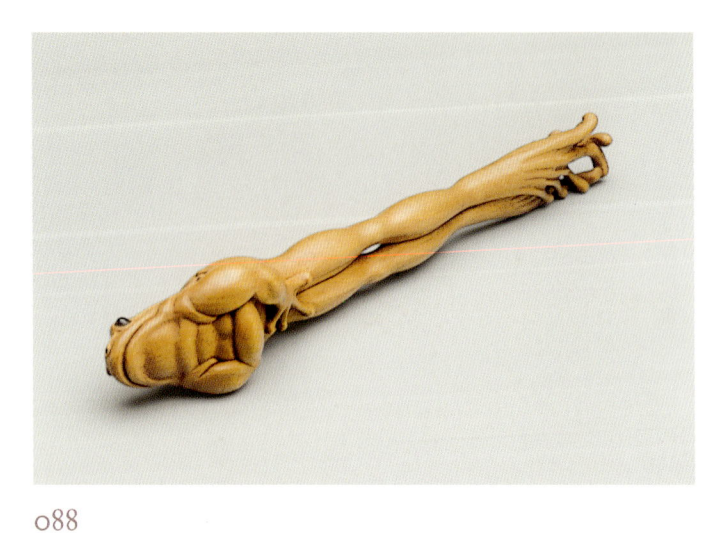

088
春乙女／Spring Virgin
黄楊／boxwood
14.7cm

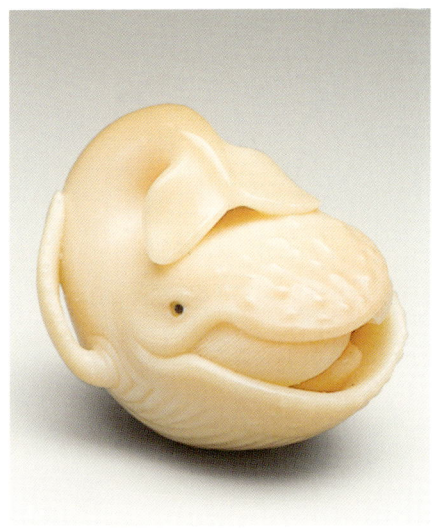

089
流れ星／Shooting Star
タグアナッツ／tagua nut
3.8cm

090
大海原／The Vast Ocean
タグアナッツ／tagua nut
4.1cm

眠れぬ夜には羊を数える。よく見ると毛糸に沿ってたくさんの羊が並んでいる。

On sleepless nights, one counts sheep. Here the artist has hidden many tiny sheep in the yarn.

091
眠れぬ夜に／Sleepless Nights
ブライアー，鹿角／briar, stag antler
4.3cm

空　哉 KUYA

092
獅子舞／Lion Dance
象牙／ivory
4.6cm

093
だるま／Daruma
黄楊／boxwood
2.2cm

MASAHIRO 昌　寛

094
虎／Tiger
マホガニー／mahogany
5.4cm

正　美　MASAMI

095
瓦にねずみ／Rats on Tile
黄楊／boxwood
4.7cm

096
眠り猫／Sleeping Cat
黄楊／boxwood
4.5cm

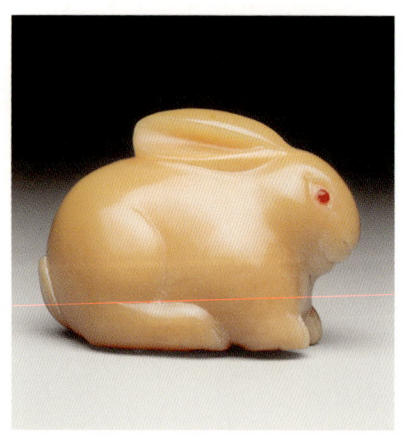

097
兎／Rabbit
タグアナッツ／tagua nut
4.1cm

098
小猿, 〔緒締〕柿(高木喜峰作)／Baby Monkey, 〔*ojime*〕Persimmon (by Kiho)
タグアナッツ, 〔緒締〕銅, 銀／tagua nut, 〔*ojime*〕copper, silver
4.2cm／1.4cm

099
草鞋に蛇／Snake on Sandal
黄楊／boxwood
4.8cm

100
申／Monkey
黄楊／boxwood
3.9cm

雅　俊　MASATOSHI

101

土龍／Mole
黒檀／ebony
6.4cm

実に見事な毛彫りが全身にほどこされている。
The carving of the fur is truly detailed and real.

102

猪蛇／Boar and Snake
黒檀／ebony
4.5cm

103

獅子舞／Lion Dance
象牙，水牛角／ivory, buffalo horn
2.3cm

MASAYUKI 祐之

104
金魚／Goldfish
蒔絵，琥珀／*maki-e*, amber
4.3cm

105
蛍／Fireflies
蒔絵，琥珀／*maki-e*, amber
4.4cm

正行 MASAYUKI

106
心ノ鍵／Key to My Heart
黄楊／boxwood
4.2cm

縄の「心」という字。裏に錠がかかっている。
The rope is shaped into the Chinese character for heart. At the back, there is a lock.

MEIGYOKUSAI 明玉斎

小野道風は書家として行き詰っているある雨の日、柳に何度も跳び付こうとしている蛙を見て、あきらめずに目標を目指す努力の尊々さに気づく。

Ono-no-Tofu, a famous calligrapher, realizes the importance of continuing to try hard when he sees a frog trying again and again to leap up onto a willow branch.

107
小野道風／Ono-no-Tofu
象牙／ivory
6.3cm

108
ネズミにローソク／Rat with Candle
象牙／ivory
3.0cm

明 幹 MEIKAN

109
風船かずらに蜻蛉／Dragonfly on Balloon Vine
マンモス牙，珊瑚／mammoth tusk, coral
5.3cm

110
初秋／Early Autumn
象牙／ivory
4.4cm

MEISHU 明 秀

111
親子蝸牛／Snail Mother and Young
象牙，琥珀／ivory, amber
4.6cm

113
蝦蟇蛙／Toads
犀角／rhinoceros horn
4.5cm

112
カブト虫／Beetles
黄楊，象牙，鼈甲／boxwood, ivory, tortoiseshell
7.4cm

115

藍　青　RANJO

114
燕舞／Swallow Dance
象牙／ivory
5.7cm

珍しい題材。子どものいたずらに母カンガルーは頭を抱える。

An unusual subject. The mischievous baby kangaroo causes his mother to hold her head in horror.

115
悪戯っ子／Naughty Boy
象牙／ivory
5.4cm

RYOSEI 梁　生

116
立雛（一対）／Pair of Hina Dolls
象牙／ivory
5.9cm／5.0cm

綾泉 RYOSEN

117

酔人 / Drunken Man
象牙 / ivory
3.7cm

RYOSHU II　良　舟（二代）

118
雛燕／Swallows' Nest
象牙／ivory
2.5cm

119
栗／Chestnuts
象牙／ivory
3.5cm

良　舟（三代）　RYOSHU III

120
草枕／Grass Pillow
象牙／ivory
5.8cm

121
おたまじゃくし／Tadpole
象牙／ivory
1.9cm

RYU 龍

122
知らぬが仏／Better Not to Know
結寿（ユス）の木／*Distylium racemosum*
4.4cm

柳　之　RYUSHI

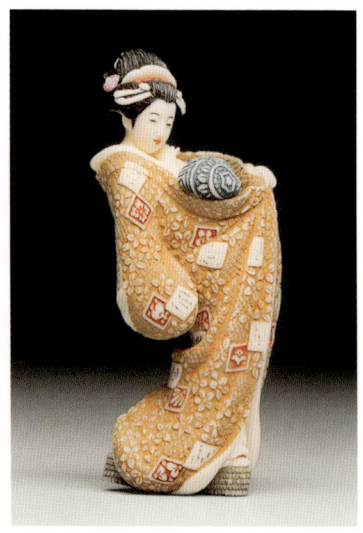

123
お願い/Please...
象牙/ivory
7.8cm

作家は美人根付で定評がある。人物の中でも、美人を彫るのは極めて難しいとされている。
Considered by many to be the leading artist in the carving of beautiful women.

124
夕霧/Evening Mist
象牙/ivory
5.6cm

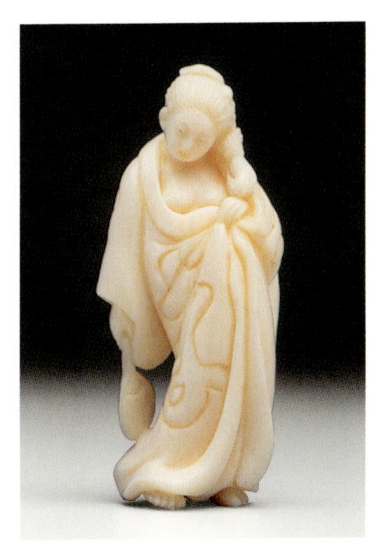

125
湯上がり／After Bathing
象牙／ivory
3.1cm

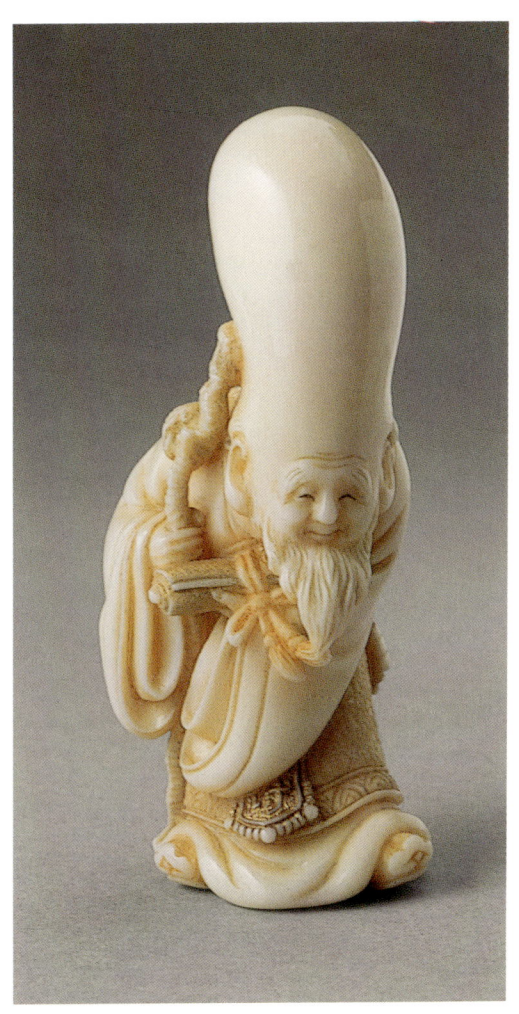

126
福禄寿／Fukurokuju
象牙／ivory
5.2cm

佐和子 SAWAKO

127
やまね／Dormouse
象牙／ivory
2.0cm

SEIHO　声　方

128
　鶴／Crane
　象牙／ivory
　1.7cm

129
　ピーマンにてんとう虫／Ladybird on Sweet Pepper
　象牙／ivory
　3.4cm

125

130

ほおずき／Ground Cherry
象牙，珊瑚，海松／ivory, coral, black coral
2.9cm

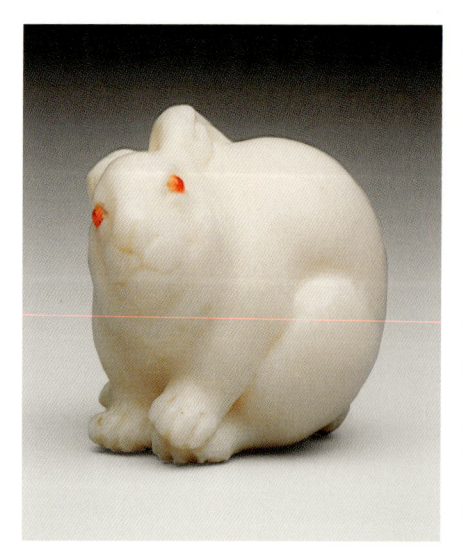

131

うさぎ／Rabbit
象牙／ivory
2.4cm

132

福禄寿／Fukurokuju
黄楊／boxwood
4.2cm

SEISUI 清 水

133
ねずみ／Mice
黄楊／boxwood
4.3cm

仙 歩　SENPO

134
飛ぶ梟／**Flying Owl**
象牙／ivory
4.5cm

135
荒城の月／
Moon Over the Ruined Castle
鹿角，青貝／stag antler, shell
3.5cm

鹿角の外皮を残し荒れた城跡を表現。横に光る三日月が青貝で象嵌され、底面にはキリギリスが彫られている（芭蕉の句「無残やな兜の下のきりぎりす」からの連想とのこと）

The natural colors of the stag antler are used to show the desolation of the castle ruins. There is a crescent moon in shell on the side and a cricket underneath.

136
盆栽鉢に蛙／**Frog in Bonsai Pot**
象牙／ivory
4.1cm

137
 やどかり／Hermit Crab
 象牙／ivory
 4.8cm

138
 土に還る／Return to the Earth
 マンモス牙／mammoth tusk
 4.5cm
 死んで腐りつつある雀の子。輪廻転生。
 A dead and decaying baby sparrow. Samsara.

139
 狼／Wolf
 象牙／ivory
 5.9cm

親 月 SHINGETSU

140
兎／Rabbit
河馬歯／hippopotamus tooth
3.3cm

141
兎／Rabbit
マンモス牙／mammoth tusk
3.9cm

142
栗／Chestnuts and Acorn
マンモス牙／mammoth tusk
3.7cm

143
てんとう虫／Ladybird
象牙／
3.7cm

SHINICHIRO 新一郎

144
明日／Tomorrow
タグアナッツ／tagua nut
3.5cm

親 良 SHINRYO

145
子／Mouse
象牙／ivory
2.8cm

146
穿山甲／Pangolins
象牙／ivory
4.1cm

SHINZAN 信山

147
かたつむり／Snails
象牙／ivory
4.3cm

静 SHIZUKA

148
子雀たち／Baby Sparrows
黄楊／boxwood
3.4cm

149
稲雀／Rice Sparrow
黄楊／boxwood
4.3cm

150
稲雀／Rice Sparrow
黄楊／boxwood
3.1cm

SHOGETSU 松　月

151

老婆／Old Woman
象牙／ivory
4.0cm

昇　己　SHOKO

152

不思議な僧／Mysterious Priest
木／wood
4.1cm

写真では見えないが奇怪な頭をした仏僧の後頭部に小さな獏が食らいついている。
Not visible in the photograph, there is a tiny *baku* biting into the back of this strange priest's head.

SHUHO 秀 方

153
薔薇／Rose
象牙／ivory
4.5cm

154
ほおずき／Ground Cherry
象牙／ivory
4.1cm

155
犬張子／Toy Dog
象牙／ivory
2.2cm

藻　水　SOSUI

156
群盲撫象図／Blind Men Touching an Elephant
木刻／wood
4.5cm

多くの盲人が象を撫でて、それぞれ自分の手に触れた部分だけで巨大な象を評している図柄。大きなものを批評しても単に部分的なものに留まり、全体像を見渡すことが出来ない事の例えを根付で表現。

A group of blind people are judging the shape of the elephant from what they can feel. It is a good rendition of a Buddhist concept that an individual is rarely capable of seeing or understanding the whole picture of something that is big.

SUMI 澄

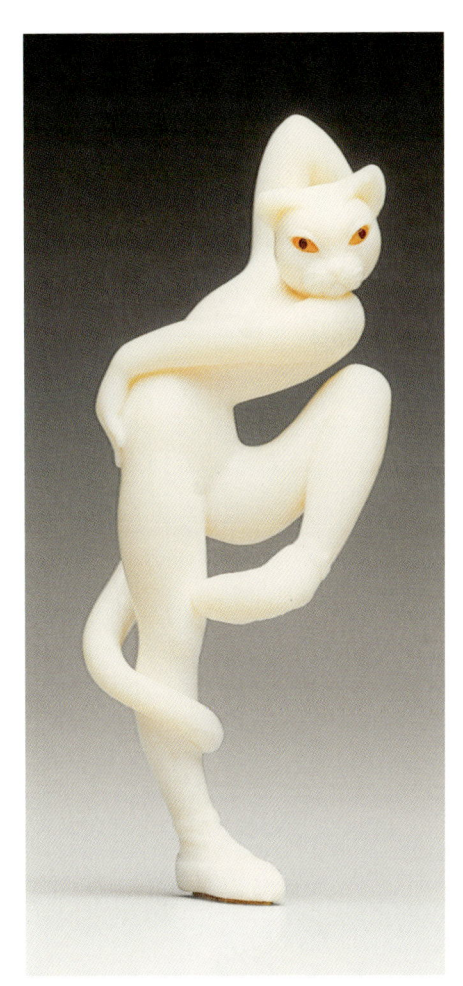

157
倫敦の猫／London Cat
象牙／ivory
7.2cm

158
河童／Kappa
マンモス牙／mammoth tusk
3.2cm

159
冬の森／Winter Forest
象牙／ivory
4.3cm

139

忠　仙　TADAHISA

160

あさり／Short-necked Clam
黄楊／boxwood
3.7cm

TADAKUMO 忠 雲

161
今は我慢／Holding Back
黄楊／boxwood
3.3cm
蝦蟇口がお金を使わないよう、自分で我慢しているところ。
Humorous portrayal of a purse keeping control of itself.

141

忠　峰　TADAMINE

162
鼠／Rat
黄楊／boxwood
2.4cm

163
腹持ち布袋／Hotei with Big Belly
黄楊／boxwood
4.0cm

164
万年／Turtle
黄楊／boxwood
4.4cm

165
龍虎／Dragon and Tiger
胡桃, 金／walnut, gold
3.5cm

166
キセル貝／Land Snail
黄楊／boxwood
5.2cm

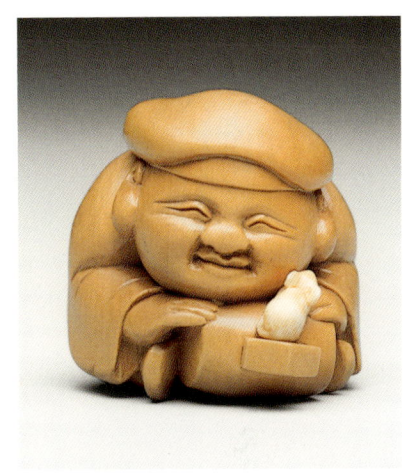

167
大黒天／Daikokuten
象牙，黄楊／ivory, boxwood
3.0cm

168
茄子，〔緒締〕木瓜／
Long Eggplant, 〔ojime〕 Japanese Quince Bud
象牙，黄楊，〔緒締〕ピンク・アイボリーウッド／
boxwood, ivory, 〔ojime〕 pink ivorywood
12.1cm／1.9cm

169
猿三番叟〔銘：矢羽〕／
Monkey Sanbaso
黄楊／boxwood
5.0cm

170

　栗鼠／Squirrel
　黄楊／boxwood
　3.3cm

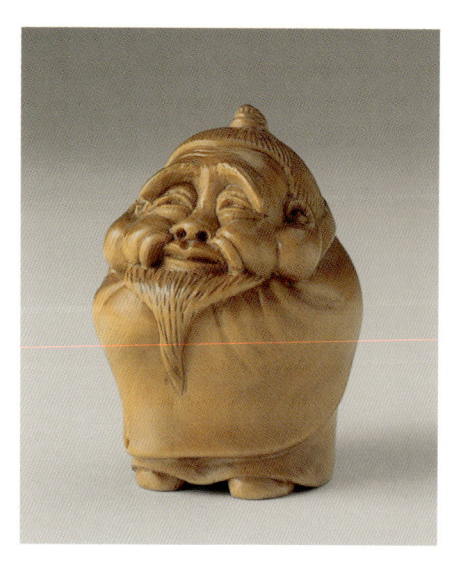

171

　寿老人／Jurojin
　黄楊／boxwood
　3.8cm

172

　弁財天／Benzaiten
　黄楊／boxwood
　3.8cm

TAMI 多美

173
うさぎ／Rabbit
象牙／ivory
4.1cm

胤　寿　TANETOSHI

174

人鳥 / Penguin
象牙，黒檀 / ivory, ebony
3.9cm

TETSURO　哲　郎

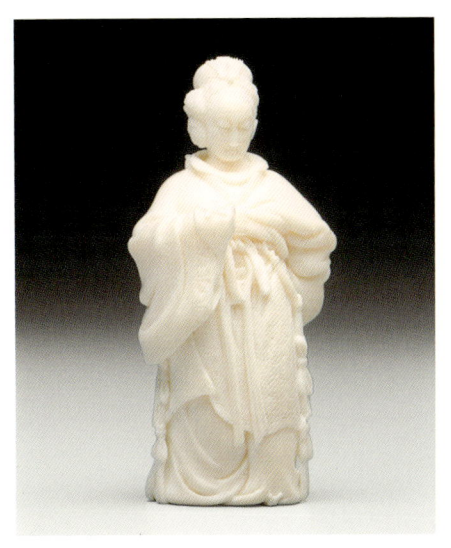

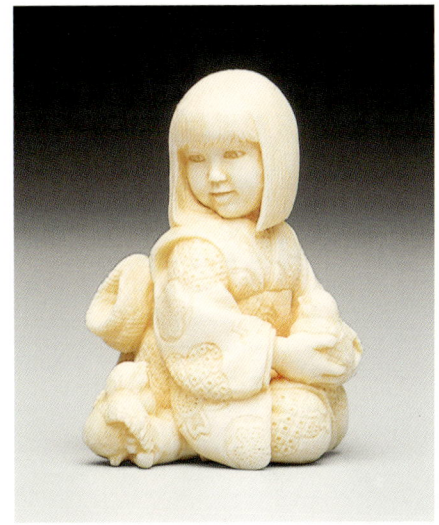

175
   唐美人／Chinese Beauty
   象牙／ivory
   5.5cm

176
   愛し／Tender Love
   象牙／ivory
   4.4cm

177
   石橋／Shakkyo
   黄楊／boxwood
   4.0cm

富　栄　TOMIE

178

魚／Stylized Fish
堆朱／*tsuishu* lacquer
8.6cm

TOSHIKI 俊晞

179
郷愁／Homesick
桜／cherry
11.0cm

濤 雲 TOUN

180
仏手柑と代代／Buddha's Hand Fruit and the "Generations"
象牙／ivory
4.5cm

仏さまの手の中に「代々」続く地球上の人類。文明がどこまで発達しても所詮仏様の手の中。己の小ささを認識し、日々感謝の心をもつことの大切さを表現。

The artist has carved a bitter orange or *dai-dai* in the Buddha's hand fruit—its name in Japanese sounds like the phrase "from generation to generation."

UNRYUAN 雲龍庵

181
鯛 / Sea Bream
蒔絵 / *maki-e*
3.7cm

182
猫 / Cat
蒔絵 / *maki-e*
3.7cm

弥　光　YAKO

183
あらい熊〔銘：朱美〕／Raccoon and Crab
象牙／ivory
3.7cm

184
待宵草／Evening Primrose
象牙／ivory
5.7cm

185
旭日〔銘：朱美〕／Rising Sun
マホガニー／mahogany
4.8cm

186
福雀〔銘：朱美〕／Good-Luck Sparrow
マホガニー／mahogany
3.5cm

187
栗鼠／Squirrel
琥珀／amber
4.2cm

保 房 YASUFUSA

188

登龍門／On the Rise
象牙／ivory
6.8cm

YOJI 洋治

189
たぬき／Badger
黄楊／boxwood
2.8cm

190
子犬／Puppy
黄楊／boxwood
3.3cm

191
亥／Wild Boar
象牙，黄楊／ivory, boxwood
4.0cm

192
福わらい／Blowfish
黄楊／boxwood
4.1cm

155

陽　佳　YOKA

193
囚われのドラゴン／Captive Dragon
マホガニー，黒檀／mahogany, ebony
5.1cm

YUKO 裕　幸

194
浮生若夢／Snail on Mushrooms
象牙／ivory
4.4cm

三昧 ZANMAI

195

梟／Owl
黄楊／boxwood
3.3cm

196

河童／Kappa
黄楊／boxwood
3.9cm

現代根付（外国人作家）
CONTEMPORARY NETSUKE (Western Artists)

Michael Birch　マイケル・バーチ

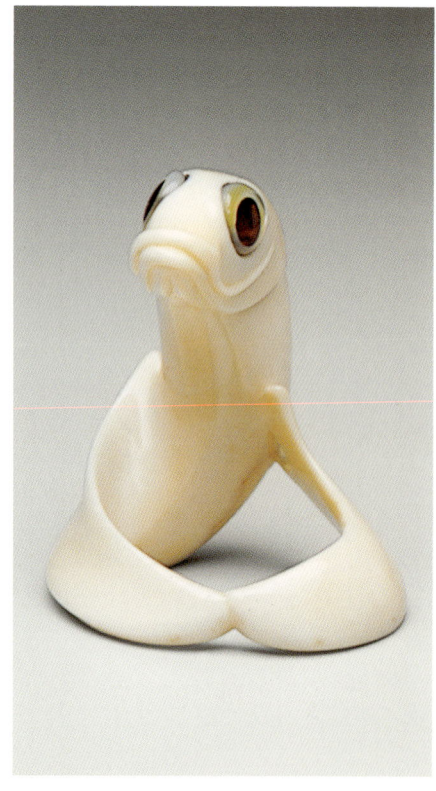

001
福禄寿／Ancestor Fukurokuju
鹿角／stag antler
4.6cm

002
鯉／Leaping Carp
イッカク牙，ルビー／narwhal tusk, ruby
3.8cm

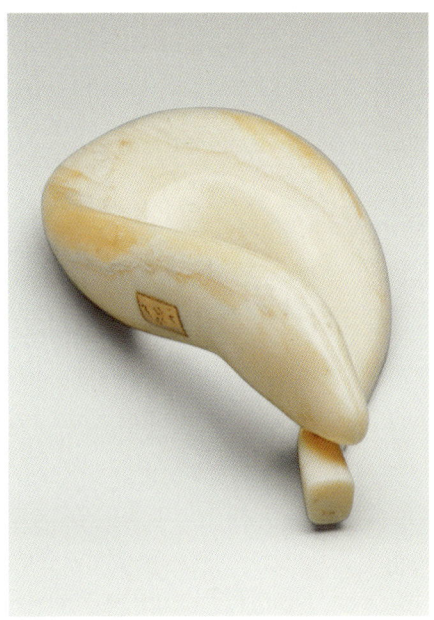

003
莢豌豆／Bean Pod
イッカク牙／narwhal tusk
14.9cm

004
馬／Horse
イッカク牙／narwhal tusk
7.2cm

005
幽霊／Lovelorn Ghost
象牙，犀角／ivory, rhinoceros horn
15.7cm

David Blissett　デーヴィッド・ブリッセット

006

蝸牛／Snail

象牙／ivory
3.5cm

ニック・ラム **Nick Lamb**

007
猪,〔緒締〕うりぼう／Wild Boar,〔*ojime*〕Baby Boars
鹿角, 黄楊,〔緒締〕黄楊, バッファロー角／stag antler, boxwood,〔*ojime*〕boxwood, buffalo horn
5.2cm／2.9cm

008
鴨／Duck
黄楊／boxwood
4.1cm

Owen Mapp オーエン・マップ

009

夢心地／Fantasy Flight
牛骨／ox-bone
8.1cm

アーミン・ミュラー　Armin Müller

010
鯉／Carps
陶器／porcelain
4.8cm

Guy Shaw ガイ・ショー

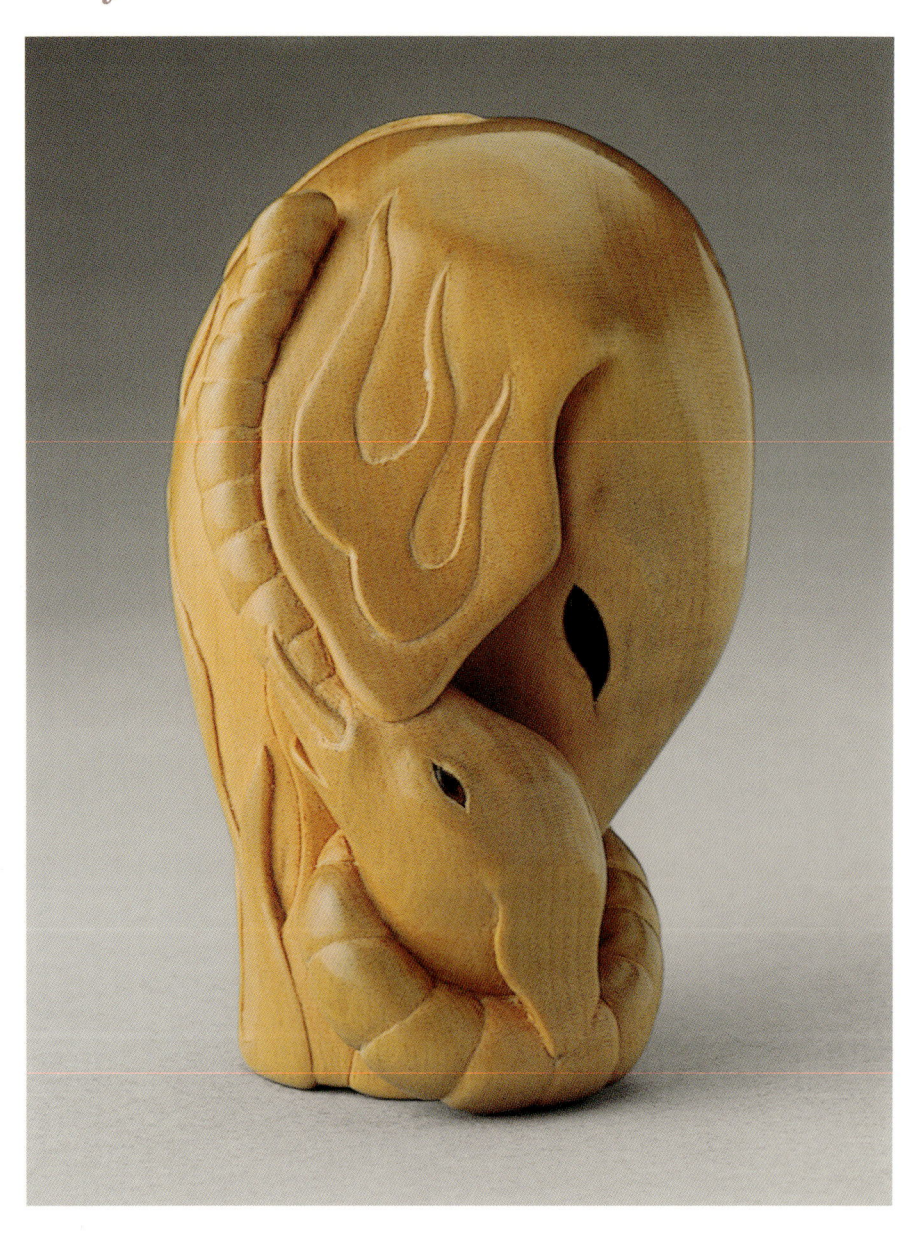

011
獏―母と子／Baku—Madonna and Child
黄楊／boxwood
5.6cm

Anthony Towne
アンソニー・タウン

012
大西洋の悪魔／Atlantic Demon
胡桃／walnut
3.1cm

Susan Wraight スーザン・レイト

013
ゾウリエビ，〔とんこつ〕ゾウリエビ，〔緒締〕魚／
Slipper Lobster, 〔*tonkotsu*〕Slipper Lobster,
〔*ojime*〕Fish
黄楊／boxwood
4.8cm
8.5cm (*tonkotsu*), 1.9cm (*ojime*)

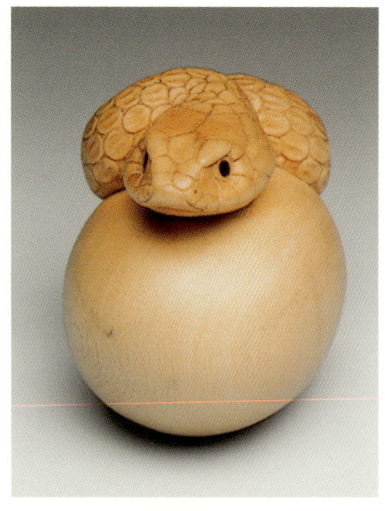

014
孵化する蛇／Hatching Snake
柊／holly
3.5cm

015
眠るヤマネ／Sleeping Dormouse
黄楊，銀／boxwood, silver
3.9cm

016
ウツボカズラ，〔緒締〕葉／Pitcher,〔ojime〕Cup
黄楊／boxwood
4.0cm／1.9cm

017
蟬，〔緒締〕脱け殻／
Cicada,〔ojime〕Cast-off Skin
黄楊／boxwood
6.7cm／3.0cm
旧キンゼイコレクション／
ex. Kinsey Collection

018
フクロネズミ／Ringtail Possum
黄楊／boxwood
4.3cm

169

019

栗／Chestnuts
柊／holly
5.0cm

020

孵化する海亀／Hatching Turtle
黄楊，タグアナッツ／boxwood, tagua nut
4.1cm

印　籠

INRO (Antique)

001

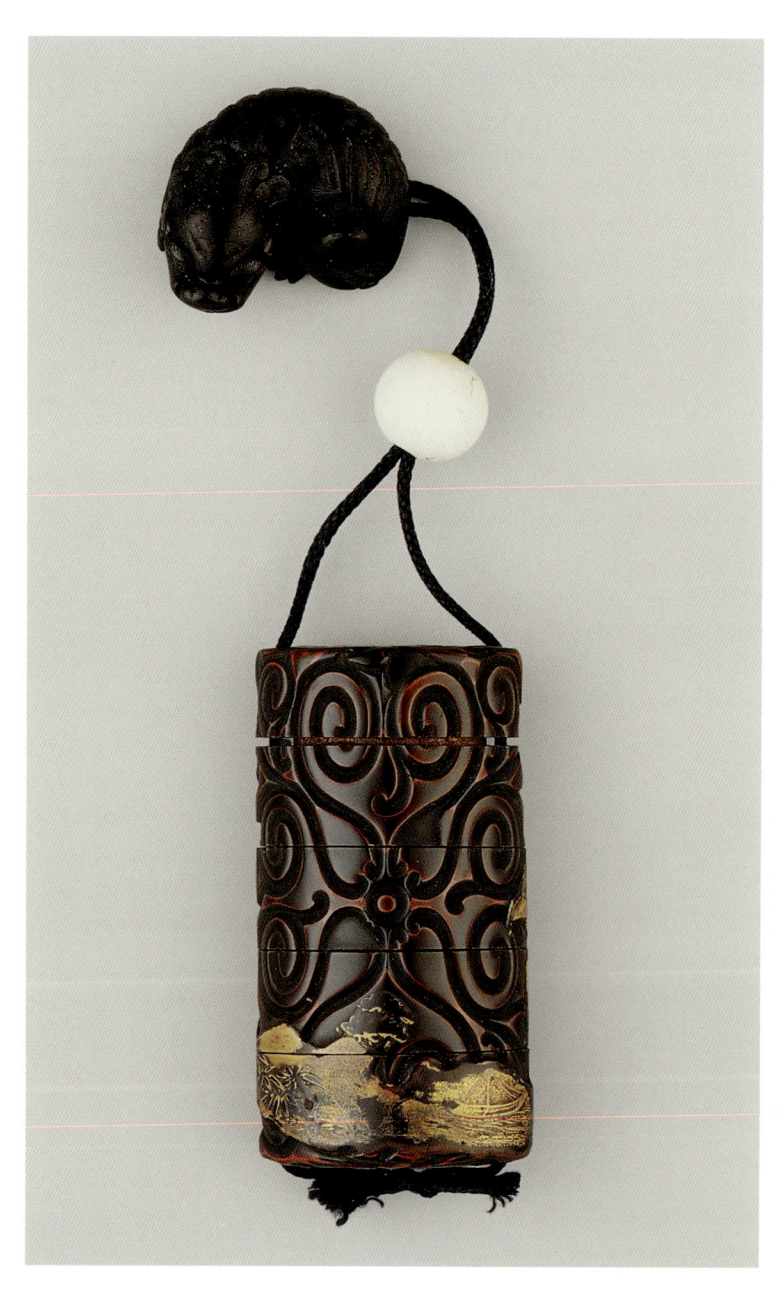

曲輪に山水図 ／ Four-case Guribori inro with maki-e landscape design, with 'Shishi' netsuke
堆漆倶利彫り，蒔絵
無銘 ／ Unsigned
印籠 7.5cm　根付（獅子）3.5cm

002

鷺八橋図／Four-case Korin-style lacquered *inro*, with *maki-e* and shell inlay, with Hermit Crab *netsuke* by Tadamine and lead *ojime* of plum flowers
蒔絵螺鈿
青々光琳造／signed Seisei-Korin zo
印籠 7.0cm　根付（やどかり／忠峰作）3.0cm　緒締（梅花 鉛）1.6cm

003

雁帆船図／Four-case lacquer *inro* with *maki-e* and lead inlay design of boat & geese, with *netsuke* of Jurojin playing 'kemari'

蒔絵，鉛象嵌
無銘／Unsigned
印籠 6.5cm　根付（象牙寿老蹴鞠）6.0cm

004
中国人物図／Four-case *tsuishu inro*, *netsuke* and *ojime* set
堆朱
無銘／Unsigned
印籠 8.0cm　根付（卵形七宝）4.0cm　緒締（曲輪）1.0cm

005

格子桐花文図 / Three-case checked design lacquer *inro* with *maki-e* pawlonia flowers
蒔絵
幸阿弥長孝　花押 / signed Koami Choko, with *kao*
印籠 6.5cm　緒締（珊瑚）0.9cm

006

蝶尽図／Four-case lacquer *inro* with *maki-e* butterfly design, with phoenix-and-turtle *netsuke* by Shoho
蒔絵
賢哉其章　花押／signed Kensai-Kisho, with *kao*
印籠 9.0cm　根付（鳳凰若松亀図／松浦作）3.7cm

007

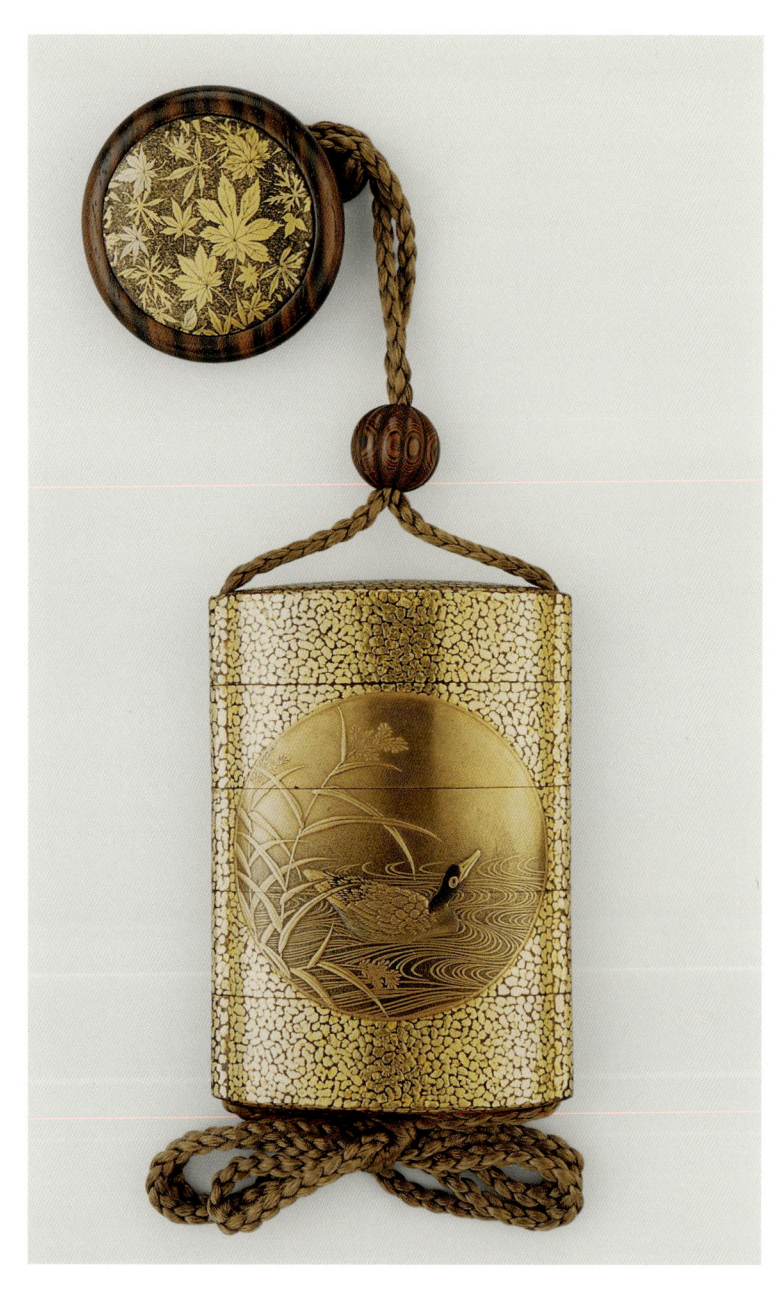

丸に雁図／Four-case lacquer *inro* with *maki-e* design of geese with *kagamibuta netsuke* of maple leaves and *tsuishu ojime*

蒔絵

常嘉斎　花押／signed Jokasai, with *kao*
印籠 8.5cm　根付（鏡蓋）4.5cm　緒締（堆朱）1.4cm

008 蔦細道図／Four-case small lacquer inro, with netsuke of a man holding a lantern by Hojitsu
蒔絵螺鈿
無銘／Unsigned
印籠 6.5cm　根付（提灯人物／法實作）4.7cm　緒締（木）1.5cm

009
亀容彫／Wooden turtle design *inro*, with *netsuke* by Bokusai and *ojime* by Tadakazu of groups of turtles
木彫
松濤／signed Shoto
印籠 7.5cm　根付（亀尽／穆斎作）2.9cm　緒締（亀／忠一作）2.0cm

O I O

牡丹に麒麟羽虎／Unusual flask-shaped lacquer *inro,* with "Moon and Turtle" *kagamibuta netsuke* and silver *ojime*

漆

無銘／Unsigned

印籠 10.5cm　根付（鏡蓋　月鼈）4.0cm　緒締（銀　柳鳥）1.0cm

OII

神馬奉納絵馬図／Four-case *togi-dashi maki-e* lacquer *inro* with shrine design of a sacred horse, with votive tablet netsuke

研出蒔絵

稲川　花押／signed Inagawa, with *kao*

印籠 6.8cm　根付（蒔絵）4.0cm　緒締（珊瑚）1.2cm

012

唐草文矢立／Silver *yatate* with *hollyhock crest* and *karakusa* design
銀
無銘／Unsigned
印籠 17.5cm　緒締(鹿角) 1.5cm

013
煙硝入形提物／Metal powder flask *sagemono*, with *fuchi-gashira* netsuke of paulownia flowers
金属
無銘／Unsigned
印籠 7.0cm　根付（桐花文縁頭）3.0cm

印　　籠（現代）

INRO (Contemporary)

001

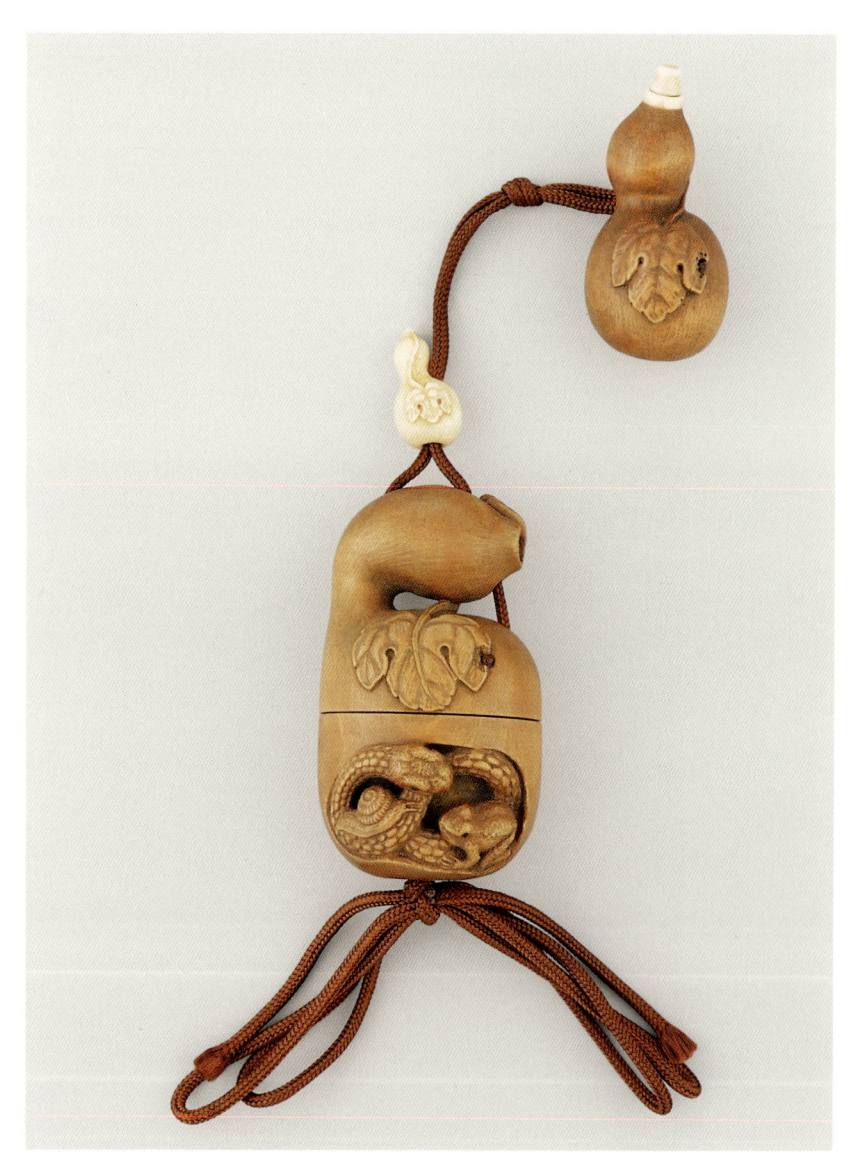

一夫（水谷数夫）／Kazuo Mizutani
〔印籠〕瓢箪に蛙，蛇，蝸牛三竦み／〔inro〕Sansukumi (frog, snake, and snail) on Gourd
黄楊／boxwood　7.0cm
〔根付〕瓢箪／〔netsuke〕Gourd
象牙，黄楊／ivory, boxwood　5.5cm
〔緒締〕瓢箪／〔ojime〕Gourd
象牙／ivory　2.4cm

002

喜峰(高木喜峰)／K IHO T AKAGI
〔トンコツ〕フライドポテト／〔*tonkotsu*〕Fried Potatoes
黄楊／boxwood　8.0cm

絹代(針谷絹代)／K INUYO H ARIYA
〔根付〕チーズバーガー／〔*netsuke*〕Cheeseburger
木，漆，貝／wood, lacquer, shell　4.0cm

〔緒締〕シェイク／〔*ojime*〕Shake
象牙，漆，アクリル／ivory, lacquer, acrylic　2.5cm

003

大下香仙／Kosen Oshita
〔印籠〕竹林／〔inro〕Bamboo Forest
黒蒔絵／black *maki-e*　7.5cm

隆（北村隆）／Takashi Kitamura
〔根付〕福良雀（青手），福良雀（染付），福良雀（赤絵金彩）
〔*netsuke*〕Good-Luck Sparrow (*ao-te*: green and yellow overglaze)
〔*netsuke*〕Good-Luck Sparrow (*some-tsuke*: cobalt underglaze)
〔*netsuke*〕Good-Luck Sparrow (*aka-e*: red overglaze with gold decoration)
陶器（九谷焼）／ceramic (Kutani)　4.5cm, 3.8cm, 4.0cm

緒　締（日本人作家）

OJIME (Japanese Artists)

美　洲 BISHU

OOI
   土龍／Mole
   黒檀／ebony
   2.6cm

KIHO　喜　峰

002

兎／Rabbits
琥珀／amber
1.6cm

003

福良雀／Good-Luck Sparrow
琥珀／amber
1.8cm

004

菊／Chrysanthemums
琥珀／amber
1.6cm

005
月に蝙蝠／Bat Circling the Moon
琥珀／amber
2.0cm

006
いるか／Dolphins
琥珀／amber
1.8cm

KINUYO 絹代

007
かくれんぼ／Playing Hide and Seek
琥珀，蒔絵／amber, *maki-e*
2.7cm

恒　山　KOZAN

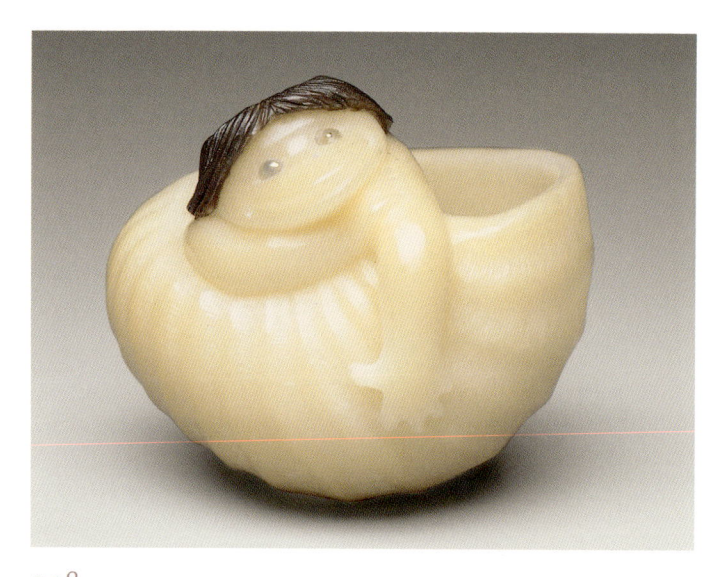

008
ゆりかご／Cradle
タグアナッツ／tagua nut
2.6cm

009
水辺／Hippopotamus
ブライアー／briar
2.2cm

MEISHU 明　秀

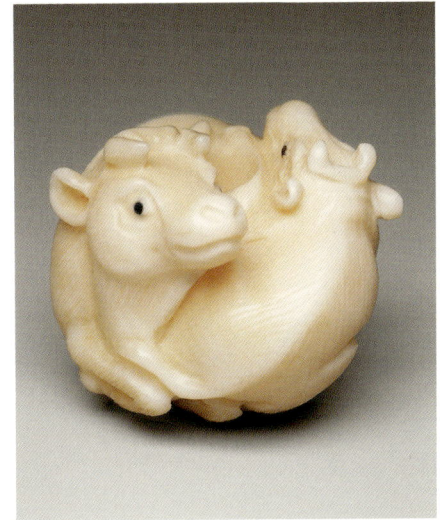

010
子／Rats
象牙／ivory
1.9cm

011
丑／Oxen
象牙／ivory
1.6cm

012
寅／Tigers
象牙／ivory
1.8cm

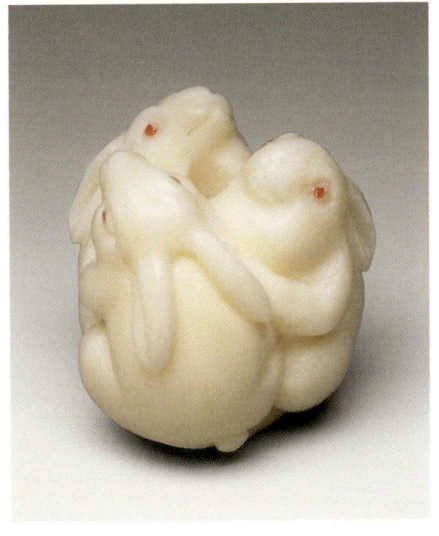

013
卯／Rabbits
象牙／ivory
1.9cm

014
辰／Dragons
象牙／ivory
1.8cm

015
巳／Snakes
象牙／ivory
1.8cm

016
午／Horses
象牙／ivory
1.8cm

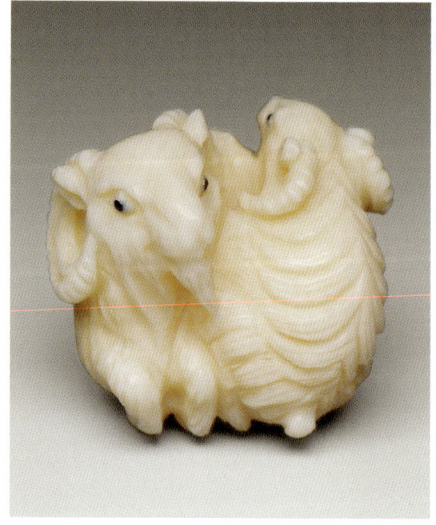

017
未／Rams
象牙／ivory
1.8cm

018

申／Monkeys
象牙／ivory
2.0cm

019

酉／Hen with Chick
象牙／ivory
1.8cm

020

戌／Dogs
象牙／ivory
1.3cm

021

亥／Boars
象牙／ivory
1.8cm

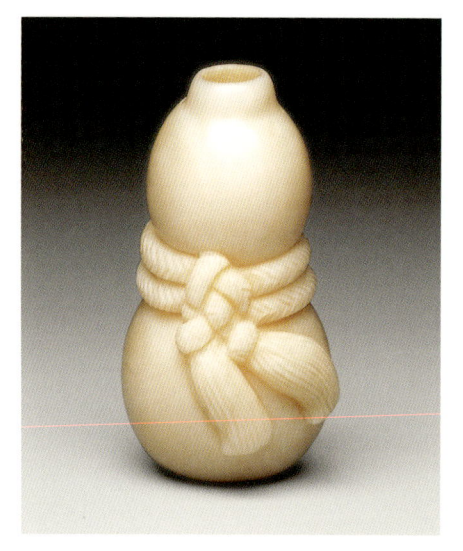

022
瓢箪／Gourd
象牙／ivory
2.1cm

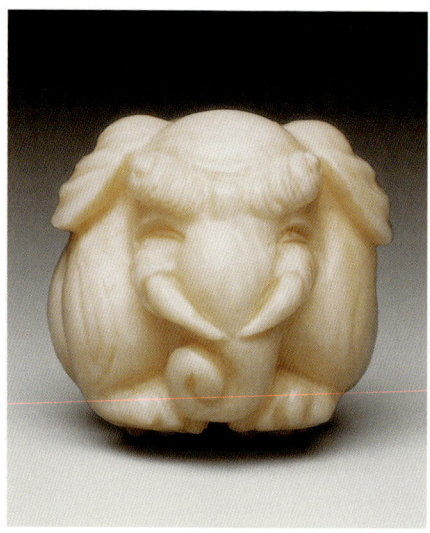

023
獏／Dream-Eating Baku
象牙／ivory
1.8cm

024
丹頂鶴／Japanese Crane
象牙，鼈甲／ivory, tortoiseshell
1.9cm

TOMIZO 富 造

025
菊／Black Chrysanthemums
象牙．黒漆／ivory, black lacquer
2.1cm

弥　　光 YAKO

026
金魚／**Goldfish**
琥珀／amber
2.0cm

緒　　締（外国人作家）
OJIME (Western Artists)

Nick Lamb ニック・ラム

001
ねずみ／Rat
黄楊／boxwood
2.1cm

002
エナガ／Long-tailed Tit
黄楊／boxwood
2.6cm

003
蛇／Tree Boa
黄楊／boxwood
2.0cm

ガイ・ショー　Guy Shaw

004
鷲づかみ／Claw
ラピス・ラズリ，アクリル／lapis lazuli, acrylic
2.3cm

作品リスト

List of Works

「凡例」

- 古根付は、テーマ分類によって収録し、その他の作品は原則として作家名のアルファベット順とした。

- 作家名は、通例に従い、日本人作家の場合は「姓・号」の順に記し、ローマ字表記では「号・姓」とし、号を大文字とした。外国人作家の場合は「名・姓」の順で記し、姓を大文字とした。作家名は、原則としてアルファベット順とした。

- 作品名は、箱書等によって作家のタイトルが確認できたものを極力採用しているが、それ以外の和文・英文タイトルについては、基本的に高円宮妃久子殿下のご指示に従った。

- 根付と緒締のセットは、根付図版に両方収めた。またその場合、「根付」・「緒締」の順にデータを記した。

- 根付・緒締が印籠に付属している場合、印籠図版に収めた。

- サイズは、最大寸法のみ記した。

[Notes]

- Antique netsuke are given by themes; other works are given in alphabetical order by the artist's names.

- Japanese artists' names are written in the order of family name and art name in Japanese, and art name and family name in English. Western artists' names are written in the order of given name and family name. Art names of Japanese artists and family names of Western artists are given in capital letters. Artists' names are listed in alphabetical order.

- Artists' original titles are given where they are known from the accompanying box (*tomobako*). In cases in which the artist's original title in either Japanese or English is unknown, titles are given on the basis of those provided by Her Imperial Highness Princess Takamado.

- When netsuke and *ojime* are illustrated as a set, both are shown in the plate for the netsuke, and the available data is given first for the netsuke and then for the *ojime*.

- When a netsuke or *ojime* is attached to an *inro*, it is illustrated in the plate for the *inro*.

- The size of each work is indicated in centimeters by its greatest dimension.

古根付 ANTIQUE NETSUKE

No.	作品名 Title	材質 Material	刻銘 Signature	サイズ Size (cm)	制作 Date	制作地域 Main Area of Activity
	動物　ANIMALS					
1	虎 Tiger Licking Its Paw	象牙 ivory	岡佳 Okatori	2.9	18th c.	京都 Kyoto
2	虎 Tiger	海象牙 marine ivory	無銘 Unsigned	2.5	19th c.	
3	親子虎 Tigress with Cub	黄楊 boxwood	岷江　花押 Minko, with *kao*	3.9	19th c.	津 Tsu
4	親子牛 Cow with Calf	象牙 ivory	友忠 Tomotada	5.1	18th c.	京都 Kyoto
5	猪 Boar	木 wood	光正　花押 Mitsumasa, with *kao*	3.5	19th c.	江戸 Edo
6	釣瓶に蛙 Frog on Bucket	黄楊 boxwood	正直(伊勢) Masanao (Ise)	3.6	19th c.	伊勢 Ise
7	石臼に蛙 Frog on Millstone	黄楊 boxwood	正直(伊勢) Masanao (Ise)	2.7	19th c.	伊勢 Ise
8	鶉 Quail	胡桃 walnut	左一山 Hidari Issan	4.2	18th c.	会津 Aizu
9	鳩 Pigeon	一位 yew	亮芳 Sukeyoshi	3.6	19th c.	飛騨 Hida
10	干鮭 Dried Salmon	鯨鬚 baleen	花押(銕哉) Tessai (*kao*)	4.1	19th c.	東京、奈良 Tokyo, Nara
	霊獣霊鳥・架空動物　SUPERNATURAL CREATURES					
11	親子獅子 Shishi with Young	黄楊 boxwood	正義 Masayoshi	4.0	19th c.	越後高田 Echigo
12	玉獅子 Shishi Holding a Ball	黒檀 ebony	正義 Masayoshi	2.7	19th c.	越後高田 Echigo
13	獅子 Shishi	木 wood	友親 Tomochika	4.1	19th c.	江戸巣鴨 Edo
14	猩々 Shojo	象牙象嵌 ivory with inlays	光雲 Koun	4.7	19th c.	
15	鬼の念仏 Oni no Nenbutsu	木，珊瑚 wood, coral	東谷 及び 銀落款 (楳立) Tokoku, with silver seal 'Bairyu'	3.0	19th c.	東京 Tokyo
16	胡瓜に河童 Kappa in Cucumber	木，翡翠 wood, jade	東谷 Tokoku	4.2	19th c.	東京 Tokyo
	故事伝説・昔話　LEGENDS AND OLD TALES					
17	蘭亭 'Rantei' Chinese Palace	黒檀 ebony	宝楽 Horaku	4.2	19th c.	京都 Kyoto
18	西王母 Seiobo Inside a Peach	鉄刀木，象牙 ironwood, ivory	景利 Kagetoshi	3.2	19th c.	京都 Kyoto
19	蘆生の夢 The Dream of Lu Sheng	紫檀 rosewood	景利 Kagetoshi	3.2	19th c.	京都 Kyoto
20	鍾馗と鬼(施灸図) Shoki and Oni	木 wood	壽玉 Jugyoku	5.0	19th c.	江戸南豊島 郡東大久保 Edo

No.	作品名 Title	材質 Material	刻銘 Signature	サイズ Size (cm)	制作 Date	制作地域 Main Area of Activity
21	鍾馗 Shoki	木刻彩色 painted wood	周山 Shuzan	4.5	19th c.	大阪長町 Osaka
22	達磨 Daruma with Hossu	木, 象牙 wood, ivory	東谷 Tokoku	3.3	19th c.	東京浅草馬車通 Tokyo
23	達磨 Daruma with Hossu	木刻象嵌 wood with inlays	光珉 Komin	2.7	19th c.	江戸 Edo
24	法螺貝に弁慶と烏天狗 Benkei with a Karasu-Tengu	黄楊 boxwood	無銘 Unsigned	6.5	19th c.	
25	関羽と魯粛 Kuan Yu and Lu Su	木 wood	萬寿 三月吉日 他 signed Manju, an auspicious day in March	3.6	19th c.	
26	三番叟 Sambaso Dancer	黄楊, 象牙 boxwood, ivory	法實 Hojitsu	3.9	19th c.	東京小石川原町鶏聲ケ窪 Tokyo
27	面遊び Boy with Fox Mask	木, 象牙 wood, ivory	法實 Hojitsu	3.2	19th c.	東京 Tokyo
28	大黒に唐子 Daikoku and Karako	象牙 ivory	長雲斎 及び 落款(秀親) Chounsai, with seal 'Hidechika'	3.5	19th c.	
29	布袋に唐子 Hotei with Karako	木, 象牙 wood, ivory	東谷 Tokoku	4.0	19th c.	東京 Tokyo
30	月に兎 Lunar Hare	象牙 ivory	重正 Shigemasa	3.5	19th c.	
31	白蔵主 Hakuzosu (Fox-Priest)	木刻彩色 painted wood	周山 Shuzan	5.4	19th c.	大阪長町 Osaka
32	葛の葉 Kuzu no Ha	木 wood	正一 Masakazu	3.8	19th c.	中京 Chukyo
33	酔いどれ狸 Drunken Badger	木 wood	北哉 Hokusai	2.7	19th c.	東京 Tokyo
34	孟宗 Meng Tsung in a Bamboo Shoot	木 wood	正次 Masatsugu	5.4	19th c.	

人物　HUMAN FIGURES

No.	作品名 Title	材質 Material	刻銘 Signature	サイズ Size (cm)	制作 Date	制作地域 Main Area of Activity
35	蹴鞠人物 Kemari Players	象牙 ivory	無銘 Unsigned	3.8	19th c.	
36	茶人 Tea Master	茶木刻彩色 painted tea-plant wood	落款銘 Signed	3.8	19th c.	
37	茶筅売 Tea-whisk Vendor	木, 象牙 wood, ivory	粛斎 Shukusai	4.0	19th c.	
38	宇治人形 Tea-leaf Picker (Uji doll)	茶木彩色 painted tea-plant wood	落款(楽之軒) Rakushiken (Seal)	3.4	19th c.	京都(宇治) Kyoto (Uji)
39	宇治人形―雨中 Tea-leaf Picker with Raincoat (Uji doll)	茶木彩色 painted tea-plant wood	落款(楽之軒) Rakushiken (Seal)	3.4	19th c.	京都(宇治) Kyoto (Uji)
40	立雛 Tachibina Doll	木刻彩色 painted wood	落款銘 Signed	5.2	19th c.	

No.	作品名 Title	材質 Material	刻銘 Signature	サイズ Size (cm)	制作 Date	制作地域 Main Area of Activity
その他 OTHERS							
41	波図色絵瓢箪 Gourd	磁器，銀 porcelain, silver	無銘 Unsigned	5.0	19th c.	平戸 Hirato
42	炭点前 Charcoal basket	木 wood	玉山 Gyokuzan	3.1	19th c.	
面根付 MASK NETSUKE							
43	能面「黒髭」 Noh mask "Kurohige"	木 wood	天下一　出目左満 Tenkaichi, Deme Saman	4.3	19th c.	
鏡蓋根付 KAGAMIBUTA NETSUKE							
44	重陽菊水図 Chrysanthemums	金属，鹿角 metal, stag anther	落款有 Signed	4.0	19th c.	
45	楽茶碗 Bottom of Raku Tea Bowl	鉄，鉄刀木，漆 iron, ironwood, lacquer	夏雄(刻銘)・不刋花押(金漆) Natsuo, with *kao* in gold lacquer	3.8	19th c.	京都・大阪・江戸 Kyoto/Osaka/Edo
46	雉鳴桜花図 Pheasant and Cherry Blossoms	金銀色絵，象牙 metal, ivory	無銘 Unsigned	4.6	19th c.	
饅頭根付 MANJU NETSUKE							
47	唐子に蓑亀(変わり饅頭根付) Karako with Tortoise	象牙，蒔絵 ivory, *maki-e*	民谷 Minkoku	3.8	19th c.	江戸 Edo
緒締 OJIME							
48	蝶に唐子 Karako with Butterfly	象牙 ivory	無銘(民谷) Unsigned (Minkoku)	1.3	19th c.	
小柄 KOZUKA							
49	龍 Dragon	黒檀 ebony	岷江惇徳　花押 Minko Juntoku, with *kao*	9.8	18〜19th c.	津 Tsu
50	龍 Dragon	象牙 ivory	懐玉 及び 落款〈正次〉 Kaigyoku, with seal 'Masatsugu'	9.0	19th c.	大阪 Osaka
51	四君子 Four Noble Plants	黒檀 ebony	懐玉斎 Kaigyokusai	9.7	19th c.	大阪 Osaka

現代根付(日本人作家) CONTEMPORARY NETSUKE (Japanese Artists)

No.	作家名／生年 Artist／Birth	作品名 Title	材質 Material	サイズ Size (cm)	制作 Date
1	佐々木明美／1959年〜 AKEMI Sasaki／b. 1959	枯 Fallen Leaf	黄楊 boxwood	4.5	1997
2	斎藤美洲／1943年〜 BISHU Saito／b. 1943	九尾之狐 Nine-Tailed Fox	象牙 ivory	4.0	1986
3		峯上 At the Summit	象牙 ivory	4.5	1987

No.	作家名／生年 Artist／Birth	作品名 Title	材質 Material	サイズ Size (cm)	制作 Date
4		獲物 Game	象牙 ivory	4.8	1989
5		玉兎 Jewel Rabbit	象牙 ivory	3.5	1982
6		日本之形　虎 Tiger	マホガニー mahogany	6.8	1991
7		鼠，〔緒締〕ねずみ Rat, 〔ojime〕Rat	黒檀，〔緒締〕マホガニー ebony, 〔ojime〕mahogany	3.5 3.1	1992
8		猪，〔緒締〕猪 Wild Boar 〔ojime〕Wild Boar	マホガニー，〔緒締〕黒檀 mahogany, 〔ojime〕ebony	5.4 3.2	1993
9	後藤雅峯／1934年～ GAHO Goto／b. 1934	ごっつぁんです 〔緒締〕米俵，塩籠 Sumo Wrestler 〔ojime〕Rice Bale, Salt Basket	河馬歯，〔緒締〕河馬歯 hippopotamus tooth 〔ojime〕hippopotamus tooth	5.6	1990
10		猛暑 Dog Days	象牙 ivory	4.2	1992
11	阿部悟堂／1914～2005年 GODO Abe／1914-2005	蛙の口ジャンケン Games Frogs Play	象牙 ivory	2.7	1986
12		我が年 My Year	象牙 ivory	3.2	1987
13	鈴木玉昇／1926年～ GYOKUSHO Suzuki／ b. 1926	猿 Monkey and Young	象牙 ivory	4.2	1989
14		碁打ち Go Player	象牙 ivory	3.1	ca.1976
15	田中治彦／1946年～ HARUHIKO Tanaka／ b. 1946	無題 Untitled	石，18金，ルビー stone, 18K gold, ruby	3.7	1992
16		無題（Ⅱ） Untitled	瑪瑙，18金 agate, 18K gold	3.4	1998
17	赤木英文／1949年～ HIDEFUMI Akagi／ b. 1949	どんこ Donko-Fish	黄楊 boxwood	6.0	1996
18	関沢芳堂／1929年～ HODO Sekizawa／b. 1929	きのこ狩り Mushroom Hunt	鹿角 stag antler	5.2	1994
19	宮沢宝泉／1942年～ HOSEN Miyazawa／ b. 1942	しめじ茸 Shimeji Mushrooms	象牙 ivory	3.3	1995
20		春の七草，〔緒締〕土鍋 Seven Spring Herbs 〔ojime〕Earthenware Pot	象牙，〔緒締〕象牙 ivory, 〔ojime〕ivory	4.3 1.9	2000
21		達磨大師 Daruma	象牙 ivory	4.1	1998
22		蛸 Octopus	象牙 ivory	5.1	1996
23	山形芳朱／1932年～ HOSHU Yamagata／ b. 1932	達磨 Daruma	象牙 ivory	2.5	1988
24		達磨 Daruma	象牙 ivory	2.1	1989
25	桜井一桜／1923～2003年 ICHIO Sakurai／1923-2003	姫だるま Hime-Daruma	象牙 ivory	4.8	1992
26	糟谷一空／1949年～ IKKU Kasuya／b. 1949	月うさぎ Moon Rabbit	象牙，鼈甲 ivory, tortoiseshell	2.7	1989

No.	作家名／生年 Artist／Birth	作品名 Title	材質 Material	サイズ Size (cm)	制作 Date
27		こうもり Bat	マホガニー mahogany	5.3	1996
28	安藤五十治／1956年～ ISOJI Ando／b. 1956	桜花 Cherry Blossoms	象牙，金蒔絵 ivory, gold *maki-e*	4.1	1992
29	岸　一舟／1917年～ ISSHU Kishi／b. 1917	羽衣 Hagoromo	象牙 ivory	5.5	1988
30		熊野 Yuya	象牙 ivory	5.1	1991
31		面尽くし Noh Masks	象牙 ivory	5.2	1993
32	桑原　仁／1956年～ JIN Kuwahara／b. 1956	新巻鮭 Salted Salmon	象牙 ivory	5.0	2000
33		早春 Early Spring	象牙 ivory	6.3	2002
34		栗 Chestnut	象牙 ivory	3.8	2002
35		干しやまめ Dried Trout	象牙 ivory	10.5	2000
36	梨本寿光／1952～2005年 JUKO Nashimoto／ 1952-2005	海豚 Dolphin	象牙 ivory	2.4	1987
37		太古の夢 Ancient Dreams	象牙 ivory	4.5	1990
38	小針樹生／1952年～ JUSHO Kobari／b. 1952	菩薩面 Bodhisattva	象牙 ivory	3.8	1997
39		裸婦 Nude	象牙 ivory	6.0	1998
40	立原寛玉／1944年～ KANGYOKU Tachihara／ b. 1944	安心して Relax	象牙 ivory	5.1	1991
41		どおり外のことも有るネ！ Strange Things Do Happen!	ヘラ鹿角 moose antler	3.3	1992
42		いななく Neighing Horse	象牙 ivory	2.6	1992
43		たねうま Seed Horse	タグアナッツ，鼈甲 tagua nut, tortoiseshell	4.0	1994
44		鯨 Whale	象牙 ivory	4.8	1995
45		見えるの　つぎの世紀 Seeing the 21st Century	象牙 ivory	4.2	2000
46		幻兎 Surrealistic Rabbit	象牙 ivory	4.1	1971
47	蝦名寛弘／1921～1998年 KANKO Ebina／ 1921-1998	犬 Dog	象牙 ivory	2.9	1991
48		子犬 Puppy	象牙 ivory	2.9	1994
49	若林寛水／1955年～ KANSUI Wakabayashi／ b. 1955	猿 Monkey	象牙 ivory	4.3	1996
50		子しし Baby Shishi	マホガニー，アクリル mahogany, acrylic	4.0	2000
51		午 Horse	象牙 ivory	4.6	2002

No.	作家名／生年 Artist／Birth	作品名 Title	材質 Material	サイズ Size (cm)	制作 Date
52	水谷一夫／1932年〜 KAZUO Mizutani／ b. 1932	碁盤に煙草入れ Go-Board with Pipe Case	象牙，黄楊，海松 ivory, boxwood, black coral	3.5	1990
53	阿部賢次／1947年〜 KENJI Abe／b. 1947	親子 Mother and Child	象牙，紫檀 ivory, rosewood	4.5	1984
54		河童 Kappa	象牙，鼈甲 ivory, tortoiseshell	4.1	1986
55		亥 Boar	象牙 ivory	3.9	1984
56		鶏，〔緒締〕鶏 Rooster, 〔ojime〕 Hen	琥珀，〔緒締〕琥珀 amber, 〔ojime〕 amber	4.7 2.1	1988
57		莢豌豆 Bean Pod	象牙 ivory	5.3	1998
58	高木喜峰／1957年〜 KIHO Takagi／b. 1957	かちかち山 Kachi-Kachi Yama	黄楊，銀，銅 boxwood, silver, copper	4.5	1995
59		草薙の剣 Kusanagi no Tsurugi	檜 Japanese cypress	4.8	2000
60		とおせんぼ You're in My Way	タグアナッツ，金 tagua nut, gold	3.8	1993
61		遠い日の夢 Dreams of Long Ago	黒檀，水晶，金 ebony, crystal, gold	5.7	1995
62		おにぎり 〔緒締〕柿 Rice-Ball 〔ojime〕 Persimmon	マンモス牙，銅 〔緒締〕銅，銀 mammoth tusk, copper 〔ojime〕 copper, silver	3.8 1.5	1993
63		かいこ Silkworm	象牙，黒檀 ivory, ebony	8.0	1992
64		宇宙観 Universe	マカデミアナッツ，銀 macadamia nut, silver	3.0	2000
65		阿吽 Beginning and End	琥珀，象牙，銀 amber, ivory, silver	4.6	1995
66		火の鳥 Firebird	琥珀，金 amber, gold	3.7	1995
67		チェシャーネコ Cheshire Cat	象牙，琥珀 ivory, amber	3.7	1997
68		不思議の国 Wonderland	黄楊，琥珀，銀 boxwood, amber, silver	4.4	1997
69		創世の時 The Beginning of Time	黒檀，金 ebony, gold	3.6	1999
70		名勝負 Good Match	象牙 ivory	3.1	2001
71		壺中天有 The Paradise Within	琥珀，銅，銀 amber, copper, silver	3.6	1998
72		悟空 The Monkey King	黄楊，金 boxwood, gold	3.8	1994
73		つくも Tsukumo (yokai spirit)	鹿角 stag antler	5.1	2000
74		毛づくろい Grooming	象牙，プラチナ，金 ivory, platinum, gold	4.0	1995
75		一人旅 Lone Journey	象牙 ivory	3.6	2001

No.	作家名／生年 Artist／Birth	作品名 Title	材質 Material	サイズ Size (cm)	制作 Date
76		金烏玉兎 Golden Crow, Silver Rabbit	琥珀，銀 amber, silver	3.3	2002
77	河瀬欽水／1925年〜 KINSUI Kawase／b. 1925	御頭 Lion-Dance Head	黄楊 boxwood	2.9	1992
78		花茄子 Eggplants with Frog	黄楊 boxwood	4.4	1996
79	針谷絹代／1959年〜 KINUYO Hariya／b. 1959	地球儀 〔緒締〕地球儀 Globe 〔ojime〕Globe	蝶貝螺鈿，金蒔絵 〔緒締〕蝶貝螺鈿，金蒔絵 mother-of-pearl, gold *maki-e* 〔*ojime*〕mother-of-pearl, gold *maki-e*	3.0 2.0	1995
80		メロン Melon	黄楊，蒔絵 boxwood, *maki-e*	3.5	1996
81		手鞠 Silk Ball	黄楊，蒔絵 boxwood, *maki-e*	3.4	1996
82		あっち行け Go Away!	タグアナッツ，蒔絵 tagua nut, *maki-e*	4.3	1997
83		花手まり Flower Ball	黄楊，蒔絵 boxwood, *maki-e*	3.4	1997
84		空の散歩 〔緒締〕太陽 Sky Promenade 〔*ojime*〕Sun	琥珀，漆 〔緒締〕象牙，漆 amber, lacquer 〔*ojime*〕ivory, lacquer	4.0 1.5	1998
85		鳳凰 Phoenix	琥珀，蒔絵，貝 amber, *maki-e*, shell	4.3	1998
86		秋草 Autumn Flowers	ガラス，蒔絵 glass, *maki-e*	3.9	2000
87	福山恒山／1946年〜 KOZAN Fukuyama／ b. 1946	オーロラ Aurora	マンモス牙，海松 mammoth tusk, black coral	5.2	1998
88		春乙女 Spring Virgin	黄楊 boxwood	14.7	1997
89		流れ星 Shooting Star	タグアナッツ tagua nut	3.8	1993
90		大海原 The Vast Ocean	タグアナッツ tagua nut	4.1	2001
91		眠れぬ夜に Sleepless Nights	ブライアー，鹿角 briar, stag antler	4.3	2002
92	中村空哉／1881〜1961年 KUYA Nakamura／ 1881-1961	獅子舞 Lion Dance	象牙 ivory	4.6	ca. 1950
93		だるま Daruma	黄楊 boxwood	2.2	(不明)
94	斎藤昌寛／1969年〜 MASAHIRO Saito／b. 1969	虎 Tiger	マホガニー mahogany	5.4	1993
95	阪井正美／1937年〜 MASAMI Sakai／b. 1937	瓦にねずみ Rats on Tile	黄楊 boxwood	4.7	1991
96		眠り猫 Sleeping Cat	黄楊 boxwood	4.5	1991
97		兎 Rabbit	タグアナッツ tagua nut	4.1	1993
98		小猿 〔緒締〕柿（高木喜峰作） Baby Monkey 〔*ojime*〕Persimmon (by Kiho)	タグアナッツ 〔緒締〕銅，銀 tagua nut 〔*ojime*〕copper, silver	4.2 1.3	1993

No.	作家名／生年 Artist／Birth	作品名 Title	材質 Material	サイズ Size (cm)	制作 Date
99		草鞋に蛇 Snake on Sandal	黄楊 boxwood	4.8	1993
100		申 Monkey	黄楊 boxwood	3.9	1994
101	中村雅俊／1915〜2001年 MASATOSHI Nakamura／ 1915-2001	土龍 Mole	黒檀 ebony	6.4	199?
102		猪蛇 Boar and Snake	黒檀 ebony	4.5	1974
103		獅子舞 Lion Dance	象牙，水牛角 ivory, buffalo horn	2.3	1952
104	針谷祐之／1954年〜 MASAYUKI Hariya／ b. 1954	金魚 Goldfish	蒔絵，琥珀 *maki-e*, amber	4.3	1997
105		蛍 Fireflies	蒔絵，琥珀 *maki-e*, amber	4.4	2001
106	森田正行／1952年〜 MASAYUKI Morita／ b. 1952	心ノ鍵 Key to My Heart	黄楊 boxwood	4.2	1999
107	平賀明玉斎／ 1896〜1991年 MEIGYOKUSAI Hiraga／ 1896-1991	小野道風 Ono-no-Tofu	象牙 ivory	6.3	ca. 1975
108		ネズミにローソク Rat with Candle	象牙 ivory	3.0	ca. 1975
109	庄司明幹／1936年〜 MEIKAN Shoji／b. 1936	風船かずらに蜻蛉 Dragonfly on Balloon Vine	マンモス牙，珊瑚 mammoth tusk, coral	5.3	1996
110		初秋 Early Autumn	象牙 ivory	4.4	2000
111	河原明秀／1934年〜 MEISHU Kawahara／ b. 1934	親子蝸牛 Snail Mother and Young	象牙，琥珀 ivory, amber	4.6	ca. 1987
112		カブト虫 Beetles	黄楊，象牙，鼈甲 boxwood, ivory, tortoiseshell	7.4	ca. 1987
113		蝦蟇蛙 Toads	犀角 rhinoceros horn	4.5	ca. 1978
114	篠崎藍青／1946年〜 RANJO Shinozaki／ b. 1946	燕舞 Swallow Dance	象牙 ivory	5.7	1988
115		悪戯っ子 Naughty Boy	象牙 ivory	5.4	1990
116	矢部梁生／1932年〜 RYOSEI Yabe／b. 1932	立雛（一対） Pair of Hina Dolls	象牙 ivory	5.9 5.0	1988
117	秋田綾泉／1932年〜 RYOSEN Akita／b. 1932	酔人 Drunken Man	象牙 ivory	3.7	1988
118	宮澤良舟（二代）／ 1912〜1982年 RYOSHU Miyazawa II／ 1912-1982	雛燕 Swallows' Nest	象牙 ivory	2.5	1980
119		栗 Chestnuts	象牙 ivory	3.5	ca. 1950
120	宮澤良舟（三代）／ 1949年〜 RYOSHU Miyazawa III／ b. 1949	草枕 Grass Pillow	象牙 ivory	5.8	1991
121		おたまじゃくし Tadpole	象牙 ivory	1.9	1992
122	椿井 龍／1957年〜 RYU Tsubai／b. 1957	知らぬが仏 Better Not to Know	結寿（ユス）の木 *Distylium racemosum*	4.4	2000

No.	作家名／生年 Artist／Birth	作品名 Title	材質 Material	サイズ Size (cm)	制作 Date
123	駒田柳之／1934年〜 RYUSHI Komada／b. 1934	お願い Please…	象牙 ivory	7.8	1989
124		夕霧 Evening Mist	象牙 ivory	5.6	1995
125		湯上がり After Bathing	象牙 ivory	3.1	1995
126		福禄寿 Fukurokuju	象牙 ivory	5.2	1997
127	寄金佐和子／1962年〜 SAWAKO Yorikane／ b. 1962	やまね Dormouse	象牙 ivory	2.0	1992
128	東　声方／1937〜2003年 SEIHO Azuma／ 1937-2003	鶴 Crane	象牙 ivory	1.7	1990
129		ピーマンにてんとう虫 Ladybird on Sweet Pepper	象牙 ivory	3.4	1999
130		ほおずき Ground Cherry	象牙，珊瑚，海松 ivory, coral, black coral	2.9	1994
131		うさぎ Rabbit	象牙 ivory	2.4	1995
132		福禄寿 Fukurokuju	黄楊 boxwood	4.2	1997
133	高山清水／1949年〜 SEISUI Takayama／b. 1949	ねずみ Mice	黄楊 boxwood	4.3	1996
134	小林仙歩／1919〜1994年 SENPO Kobayashi／ 1919-1994	飛ぶ梟 Flying Owl	象牙 ivory	4.5	1982
135		荒城の月 Moon Over the Ruined Castle	鹿角，青貝 stag antler, shell	3.5	1992
136		盆栽鉢に蛙 Frog in Bonsai Pot	象牙 ivory	4.1	1974
137		やどかり Hermit Crab	象牙 ivory	4.8	1982
138		土に還る Return to the Earth	マンモス牙 mammoth tusk	4.5	1993
139		狼 Wolf	象牙 ivory	5.9	1986
140	村松親月／1934年〜 SHINGETSU Muramatsu／ b. 1934	兎 Rabbit	河馬歯 hippopotamus tooth	3.3	1991
141		兎 Rabbit	マンモス牙 mammoth tusk	3.9	1991
142		栗 Chestnuts and Acorn	マンモス牙 mammoth tusk	3.7	1995
143		てんとう虫 Ladybird	象牙 ivory	3.7	1999
144	柳瀬新一郎／1969年〜 SHINICHIRO Yanase／ b. 1969	明日 Tomorrow	タグアナッツ tagua nut	3.5	1992
145	鈴木親良／1910〜1989年 SHINRYO Suzuki／ 1910-1989	子 Mouse	象牙 ivory	2.8	ca. 1988
146		穿山甲 Pangolins	象牙 ivory	4.1	1982

No.	作家名／生年 Artist／Birth	作品名 Title	材質 Material	サイズ Size (cm)	制作 Date
147	一川信山／1948年～ SHINZAN Ichikawa／ b. 1948	かたつむり Snails	象牙 ivory	4.3	1989
148	木村 静／1942年～ SHIZUKA Kimura／ b. 1942	子雀たち Baby Sparrows	黄楊 boxwood	3.4	2000
149		稲雀 Rice Sparrow	黄楊 boxwood	4.3	1997
150		稲雀 Rice Sparrow	黄楊 boxwood	3.1	2000
151	天野松月／1887～1980年 SHOGETSU Matsuno／ 1887-1980	老婆 Old Woman	象牙 ivory	4.0	ca. 1930
152	西野昇己／1915～1969年 SHOKO Nishino／ 1915-1969	不思議な僧 Mysterious Priest	木 wood	4.1	(不明)
153	八川秀方／1919年～ SHUHO Yagawa／b. 1919	薔薇 Rose	象牙 ivory	4.5	ca. 1960
154		ほおずき Ground Cherry	象牙 ivory	4.1	ca. 1960
155		犬張子 Toy Dog	象牙 ivory	2.2	1990
156	大内藻水／1911～1972年 SOSUI Ouchi／1911-1972	群盲撫象図 Blind Men Touching an Elephant	木刻 wood	4.5	(不明)
157	佐田 澄／1944年～ SUMI Sata／b. 1944	倫敦の猫 London Cat	象牙 ivory	7.2	1999
158		河童 Kappa	マンモス牙 mammoth tusk	3.2	1994
159		冬の森 Winter Forest	象牙 ivory	4.3	2002
160	弓削忠仙／1947年～ TADAHISA Yuge／ b. 1947	あさり Short-necked Clam	黄楊 boxwood	3.7	1996
161	中川忠雲／1969年～ TADAKUMO Nakagawa／ b. 1969	今は我慢 Holding Back	黄楊 boxwood	3.3	1996
162	中川忠峰／1947年～ TADAMINE Nakagawa／ b. 1947	鼠 Rat	黄楊 boxwood	2.4	1991
163		腹持ち布袋 Hotei with Big Belly	黄楊 boxwood	4.0	1995
164		万年 Turtle	黄楊 boxwood	4.4	1996
165		龍虎 Dragon and Tiger	胡桃, 金 walnut, gold	3.5	1998
166		キセル貝 Land Snail	黄楊 boxwood	5.2	1997
167		大黒天 Daikokuten	象牙, 黄楊 ivory, boxwood	3.0	1999
168		茄子 〔緒締〕木瓜 Long Eggplant 〔ojime〕Japanese Quince Bud	象牙,黄楊 〔緒締〕ピンク・アイボリーウッド boxwood, ivory 〔ojime〕pink ivorywood	12.1 1.9	1997

No.	作家名／生年 Artist／Birth	作品名 Title	材質 Material	サイズ Size (cm)	制作 Date
169		猿三番叟〔銘：矢羽〕 Monkey Sanbaso	黄楊 boxwood	5.0	1992
170		栗鼠 Squirrel	黄楊 boxwood	3.3	1989
171		寿老人 Jurojin	黄楊 boxwood	3.8	1992
172		弁財天 Benzaiten	黄楊 boxwood	3.8	1991
173	中村多美／1946〜2001年 TAMI Nakamura／ 1946-2001	うさぎ Rabbit	象牙 ivory	4.1	1993
174	平賀胤寿／1947年〜 TANETOSHI Hiraga／ b. 1947	人鳥 Penguin	象牙，黒檀 ivory, ebony	3.9	1997
175	森　哲郎／1960年〜 TETSURO Mori／b. 1960	唐美人 Chinese Beauty	象牙 ivory	5.5	1998
176		愛し Tender Love	象牙 ivory	4.4	2001
177		石橋 Shakkyo	黄楊 boxwood	4.0	1999
178	中村富栄／1925〜1993年 TOMIE Nakamura／ 1925-1993	魚 Stylized Fish	堆朱 tsuishu lacquer	8.6	1993
179	田中俊睍／1942年〜 TOSHIKI Tanaka／ b. 1942	郷愁 Homesick	桜 cherry	11.0	1995
180	宍戸濤雲／1960年〜 TOUN Shishido／b. 1960	仏手柑と代代 Buddha's Hand Fruit and the "Generations"	象牙 ivory	4.5	2002
181	北村雲龍庵／1952年〜 UNRYUAN Kitamura／ b. 1952	鯛 Sea Bream	蒔絵 maki-e	3.7	1994
182		猫 Cat	蒔絵 maki-e	3.7	1994
183	太田弥光／1947年〜 YAKO Ota／b. 1947	あらい熊〔銘：朱美〕 Raccoon and Crab	象牙 ivory	3.7	1991
184		待宵草 Evening Primrose	象牙 ivory	5.7	1999
185		旭日〔銘：朱美〕 Rising Sun	マホガニー mahogany	4.8	1992
186		福雀〔銘：朱美〕 Good-Luck Sparrow	マホガニー mahogany	3.5	1993
187		栗鼠 Squirrel	琥珀 amber	4.2	1997
188	斎藤保房／1931年〜 YASUFUSA Saito／ b. 1931	登龍門 On the Rise	象牙 ivory	6.8	2001
189	山田洋治／1934年〜 YOJI Yamada／b. 1934	たぬき Badger	黄楊 boxwood	2.8	1990
190		子犬 Puppy	黄楊 boxwood	3.3	1990
191		亥 Wild Boar	象牙，黄楊 ivory, boxwood	4.0	1998

No.	作家名／生年 Artist／Birth	作品名 Title	材質 Material	サイズ Size (cm)	制作 Date
192		福わらい Blowfish	黄楊 boxwood	4.1	1996
193	向田陽佳／1968年～ YOKA Mukaida／b. 1968	囚われのドラゴン Captive Dragon	マホガニー，黒檀 mahogany, ebony	5.1	2000
194	阿部裕幸／1952年～ YUKO Abe／b. 1952	浮生若夢 Snail on Mushrooms	象牙 ivory	4.4	1997
195	小野里三昧／1967年～ ZANMAI Onosato／ b. 1967	梟 Owl	黄楊 boxwood	3.3	2002
196		河童 Kappa	黄楊 boxwood	3.9	1999

現代根付(外国人作家) CONTEMPORARY NETSUKE (Western Artists)

No.	作家名／生年 Artist／Birth	作品名 Title	材質 Material	サイズ Size (cm)	制作 Date
1	マイケル・バーチ／ 1926年～／英国 Michael BIRCH／ b. 1926／U.K.	福禄寿 Ancestor Fukurokuju	鹿角 stag antler	4.6	1992
2		鯉 Leaping Carp	イッカク牙，ルビー narwhal tusk, ruby	3.8	1979
3		莢豌豆 Bean Pod	イッカク牙 narwhal tusk	14.9	1975
4		馬 Horse	イッカク牙 narwhal tusk	7.2	1976
5		幽霊 Lovelorn Ghost	象牙，犀角 ivory, rhinoceros horn	15.7	1976
6	デーヴィッド・ブリッセット／ 1924年～／英国 David BLISSETT／ b. 1924／U.K.	蝸牛 Snail	象牙 ivory	3.5	1994
7	ニック・ラム／1948年～／ 英国 Nick LAMB／b. 1948／ U.K.	猪 〔緒締〕うりぼう Wild Boar 〔ojime〕Baby Boars	鹿角，黄楊 〔緒締〕黄楊，バッファロー角 stag antler, boxwood 〔ojime〕boxwood, buffalo horn	5.2 2.9	1991
8		鴨 Duck	黄楊 boxwood	4.1	1996
9	オーエン・マップ／ 1945年～／ニュージーランド Owen MAPP／ b. 1945／New Zealand	夢心地 Fantasy Flight	牛骨 ox-bone	8.1	1996
10	アーミン・ミュラー／ 1942～2000年／アメリカ Armin MÜLLER／ 1942-2000／U.S.A	鯉 Carps	陶器 porcelain	4.8	2000
11	ガイ・ショー／ 1951～2003年／英国 Guy SHAW／ 1951-2003／U.K.	獏―母と子 Baku—Madonna and Child	黄楊 boxwood	5.6	1991
12	アンソニー・タウン／ 1956年～／アメリカ Anthony TOWNE／ b. 1956／U.S.A	大西洋の悪魔 Atlantic Demon	胡桃 walnut	3.1	1991
13	スーザン・レイト／ 1955年～／英国 Susan WRAIGHT／ b. 1955／U.K.	ゾウリエビ 〔とんこつ〕ゾウリエビ 〔緒締〕魚 Slipper Lobster, 〔tonkotsu〕 Slipper Lobster, 〔ojime〕Fish	黄楊 boxwood	4.8 8.5 1.9	1990 1997 1997

No.	作家名／生年 Artist／Birth	作品名 Title	材質 Material	サイズ Size (cm)	制作 Date
14		孵化する蛇 Hatching Snake	柊 holly	3.5	1993
15		眠るヤマネ Sleeping Dormouse	黄楊, 銀 boxwood, silver	3.9	1995
16		ウツボカズラ,〔緒締〕葉 Pitcher,〔*ojime*〕Cup	黄楊 boxwood	4.0 1.9	1997
17		蟬,〔緒締〕脱け殻 Cicada,〔*ojime*〕Cast-off Skin	黄楊 boxwood	6.7 3.0	1995
18		フクロネズミ Ringtail Possum	黄楊 boxwood	4.3	2002
19		栗 Chestnuts	柊 holly	5.0	1989
20		孵化する海亀 Hatching Turtle	黄楊, タグアナッツ boxwood, tagua nut	4.1	1996

印籠　INRO (Antique)

No.	作品名 Description	材質	刻銘 Signature	サイズ Size (cm)	制作 Date
1	曲輪に山水図 Four-case Guribori *inro* with *maki-e* landscape design, with 'Shishi' *netsuke*	堆漆倶利彫り, 蒔絵	無銘 Unsigned	7.5 3.5	18th c.
2	鷺八橋図 Four-case Korin-style lacquered *inro*, with *maki-e* and shell inlay, with Hermit Crab *netsuke* by Tadamine and lead *ojime* of plum flowers	蒔絵螺鈿	青々光琳造 signed Seisei-Korin zo	7.0 3.0 1.6	18th c.
3	雁帆船図 Four-case lacquer *inro* with *maki-e* and lead inlay design of boat & geese, with *netsuke* of Jurojin playing '*kemari*'	蒔絵, 鉛象嵌	無銘 Unsigned	6.5 6.0	19th c.
4	中国人物図 Four-case *tsuishu inro*, *netsuke* and *ojime* set	堆朱	無銘 Unsigned	8.0 4.0 1.0	19th c.
5	格子桐花文図 Three-case checked design lacquer *inro* with *maki-e* pawlonia flowers	蒔絵	幸阿弥長孝　花押 signed Koami Choko, with *kao*	6.5 0.9	19th c.
6	蝶尽図 Four-case lacquer *inro* with *maki-e* butterfly design, with phoenix-and-turtle *netsuke* by Shoho	蒔絵	賢哉其章　花押 signed Kensai-Kisho, with *kao*	9.0 3.7	19th c.
7	丸に雁図 Four-case lacquer *inro* with *maki-e* design of geese with *kagamibuta netsuke* of maple leaves and *tsuishu ojime*	蒔絵	常嘉斎　花押 signed Jokasai, with *kao*	8.5 4.5 1.4	19th c.
8	蔦細道図 Four-case small lacquer *inro*, with *netsuke* of a man holding a lantern by Hojitsu	蒔絵螺鈿	無銘 Unsigned	6.5 4.7 1.5	19th c.
9	亀容彫 Wooden turtle design *inro*, with *netsuke* by Bokusai and *ojime* by Tadakazu of groups of turtles	木彫	松濤 signed Shoto	7.5 2.9 2.0	19th c.

No.	作品名 Description	材質	刻銘 Signature	サイズ Size (cm)	制作 Date
10	牡丹に麒麟羽虎 Unusual flask-shaped lacquer *inro*, with "Moon and Turtle" *kagamibuta* netsuke and silver *ojime*	漆	無銘 Unsigned	10.5 4.0 1.0	不明
11	神馬奉納絵馬図 Four-case *togi-dashi maki-e* lacquer *inro* with shrine design of a sacred horse, with votive tablet netsuke	研出蒔絵	稲川　花押 signed Inagawa, with *kao*	6.8 4.0 1.2	不明
12	唐草文矢立 Silver *yatate* with *hollyhock crest* and *karakusa* design	銀	無銘 Unsigned	17.5 1.5	19th c.
13	煙硝入形提物 Metal powder flask *sagemono*, with *fuchi-gashira* netsuke of paulownia flowers	金属	無銘 Unsigned	7.0 3.0	19th c.

印籠（現代）　INRO (Contemporary)

No.	作家名／生年 Artist／Birth	作品名 Title	材質 Material	サイズ Size (cm)	制作 Date
1	一夫（水谷数夫）／ 1932年～ KAZUO Mizutani／ b. 1932	〔印籠〕瓢箪に蛙、蛇、蝸牛三竦み 〔*inro*〕Sansukumi (frog, snake, and snail) on Gourd	黄楊 boxwood	7.0	1995
		〔根付〕瓢箪 〔*netsuke*〕Gourd	象牙，黄楊 ivory, boxwood	5.5	1995
		〔緒締〕瓢箪 〔*ojime*〕Gourd	象牙 ivory	2.4	1995
2	喜峰（高木喜峰）／1957年～ KIHO Takagi／b. 1957	〔トンコツ〕フライドポテト 〔*tonkotsu*〕Fried Potatoes	黄楊 boxwood	8.0	1998
	絹代（針谷絹代）／ 1959年～ KINUYO Hariya／ b. 1959	〔根付〕チーズバーガー 〔*netsuke*〕Cheeseburger	木，漆，貝 wood, lacquer, shell	4.0	1998
		〔緒締〕シェイク 〔*ojime*〕Shake	象牙，漆，アクリル ivory, lacquer, acrylic	2.5	1998
3	大下香仙／1948年～ KOSEN Oshita／b. 1948	〔印籠〕竹林 〔*inro*〕Bamboo Forest	黒蒔絵 black *maki-e*	7.5	1996
	隆（北村隆）／ 1946年～ TAKASHI Kitamura／ b. 1946	〔根付〕福良雀（青手） 〔*netsuke*〕Good-Luck Sparrow (*ao-te*: green and yellow overglaze)	陶器（九谷焼） ceramic (Kutani)	4.5	1996
		福良雀（染付） 〔*netsuke*〕Good-Luck Sparrow (*some-tsuke*: cobalt underglaze)	陶器（九谷焼） ceramic (Kutani)	3.8	1996
		福良雀（赤絵金彩） 〔*netsuke*〕Good-Luck Sparrow (*aka-e*: red overglaze with gold decoration)	陶器（九谷焼） ceramic (Kutani)	4.0	1996

緒締（日本人作家）　OJIME (Japanese Artists)

No.	作家名／生年 Artist／Birth	作品名 Title	材質 Material	サイズ Size (cm)	制作 Date
1	斎藤美洲／1943年～ BISHU Saito／b. 1943	土龍 Mole	黒檀 ebony	2.6	1992
2	高木喜峰／1957年～ KIHO Takagi／b. 1957	兎 Rabbits	琥珀 amber	1.6	1992
3		福良雀 Good-Luck Sparrow	琥珀 amber	1.8	1992

No.	作家名／生年 Artist／Birth	作品名 Title	材質 Material	サイズ Size (cm)	制作 Date
4		菊 Chrysanthemums	琥珀 amber	1.6	1992
5		月に蝙蝠 Bat Circling the Moon	琥珀 amber	2.0	1992
6		いるか Dolphins	琥珀 amber	1.8	1994
7	針谷絹代／1959年～ KINUYO Hariya／b. 1959	かくれんぼ Playing Hide and Seek	琥珀, 蒔絵 amber, *maki-e*	2.7	1996
8	福山恒山／1946年～ KOZAN Fukuyama／ b. 1946	ゆりかご Cradle	タグアナッツ tagua nut	2.6	1993
9		水辺 Hippopotamus	ブライアー briar	2.2	1993
10	河原明秀／1934年～ MEISHU Kawahara／ b. 1934	子 Rats	象牙 ivory	1.9	1975
11		丑 Oxen	象牙 ivory	1.6	1975
12		寅 Tigers	象牙 ivory	1.8	1975
13		卯 Rabbits	象牙 ivory	1.9	1975
14		辰 Dragons	象牙 ivory	1.8	1975
15		巳 Snakes	象牙 ivory	1.8	1975
16		午 Horses	象牙 ivory	1.8	1975
17		未 Rams	象牙 ivory	1.8	1975
18		申 Monkeys	象牙 ivory	2.0	1975
19		酉 Hen with Chick	象牙 ivory	1.8	1975
20		戌 Dogs	象牙 ivory	1.3	1975
21		亥 Boars	象牙 ivory	1.8	1975
22		瓢箪 Gourd	象牙 ivory	2.1	1975
23		獏 Dream-Eating Baku	象牙 ivory	1.8	1975
24		丹頂鶴 Japanese Crane	象牙, 鼈甲 ivory, tortoiseshell	1.9	1975
25	更谷富造／1949年～ TOMIZO Saratani／ b. 1949	菊 Black Chrysanthemums	象牙, 黒漆 ivory, black lacquer	2.1	1991
26	太田弥光／1947年～ YAKO Ota／b. 1947	金魚 Goldfish	琥珀 amber	2.0	1998

緒締(外国人作家)　OJIME (Western Artists)

No.	作家名／生年 Artist／Birth	作品名 Title	材質 Material	サイズ Size (cm)	制作 Date
1	ニック・ラム／ 1948年〜／英国 Nick LAMB／ b. 1948／U.K.	ねずみ Rat	黄楊 boxwood	2.1	1991
2		エナガ Long-tailed Tit	黄楊 boxwood	2.6	1992
3		蛇 Tree Boa	黄楊 boxwood	2.0	1991
4	ガイ・ショー／ 1951〜2003年／英国 Guy SHAW／ 1951-2003／U.K.	鷲づかみ Claw	ラピス・ラズリ，アクリル lapis lazuli, acrylic	2.3	1991

作家略歴

Artists' Profiles

佐々木明美　AKEMI Sasaki

本名：森明美（1959年生）
出身地：北海道
現住所：神奈川県藤沢市
根付制作開始：1999年
主に使用している材料／材質：象牙、木材
得意とするテーマ：植物
主な仕上げ方：無着色、やしゃ染め

Actual Name: Akemi Mori (b. 1959)
Place of Birth: Hokkaido Prefecture
Current Address: Kanagawa Prefecture
Began Carving Netsuke in: 1999
Main Materials Used: Ivory, wood
Favorite Subjects: Plants
Main Types of Finish: Uncolored, *yasha* stain

箱書き落款　Signature/seal on the box 　　銘　Signature

斎藤美洲　BISHU Saito

本名：斎藤勝利（1943年生）
出身地：東京都
現住所：埼玉県川口市
根付制作開始：1961年
主に使用している材料／材質：象牙、マンモス牙、木材、鹿角、海松堆朱、琥珀など
得意とするテーマ：動物（魚介類）
主な仕上げ方：無着色、やしゃ染め、顔料着色、染料着色、漆

Actual Name: Katsutoshi Saito (b. 1943)
Place of Birth: Tokyo
Current Address: Saitama Prefecture
Began Carving Netsuke in: 1961
Main Materials Used: Ivory, mammoth tusk, wood, stag antler, black coral, lacquer, amber, etc.
Favorite Subjects: Animals
Main Types of Finish: Uncolored, *yasha* stain, paint, dyes, lacquer

箱書き落款　Signature/seal on the box 　　銘　Signature

後藤雅峰　GAHO Goto

本名：後藤雅弘（1934年生）
出身地：岐阜県
現住所：岐阜県大垣市
根付制作開始：1988年
根付制作以前／以外の仕事：印刷業
主に使用している材料／材質：象牙、木材
得意とするテーマ：人物、動物、魚介類
主な仕上げ方：やしゃ染め（顔料着色、染料着色）

Actual Name: Masahiro Goto (b. 1934)
Place of Birth: Gifu Prefecture
Current Address: Gifu Prefecture
Began Carving Netsuke in: 1988
Former/Other Occupation(s): Printer
Main Materials Used: Ivory, wood
Favorite Subjects: Human figures, animals, aquatic creatures
Main Types of Finish: *Yasha* stain (paint, dyes)

箱書き落款　Signature/seal on the box 　　銘　Signature

阿部悟堂　　GODO Abe

本名：阿部悟一郎（1914年～2005年）
出身地：栃木県
現住所：埼玉県さいたま市
根付制作期間：1929年～1984年
主に使用している材料／材質：象牙、木材
得意とするテーマ：人物、動物
主な仕上げ方：無着色、やしゃ染め、べっ甲象嵌

Actual Name: Goichiro Abe (1914-2005)
Place of Birth: Tochigi Prefecture
Current Address: Saitama Prefecture
Carved Netsuke in: 1929-1984
Main Materials Used: Ivory, wood
Favorite Subjects: Human figures, animals
Main Types of Finish: Uncolored, *yasha* stain, tortoiseshell inlay

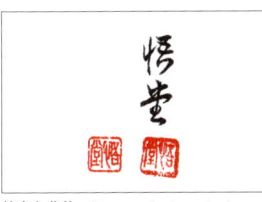

箱書き落款　Signature/seal on the box 　　　銘　Signature

鈴木玉昇　　GYOKUSHO Suzuki

本名：鈴木利雄（1926年生）
出身地：東京都
現住所：東京都北区
根付制作開始：1971年
根付制作以前／以外の仕事：象牙彫刻（置物）
主に使用している材料／材質：象牙、マンモス牙
得意とするテーマ：人物
主な仕上げ方：やしゃ染め

Actual Name: Toshio Suzuki (b. 1926)
Place of Birth: Tokyo
Current Address: Tokyo
Began Carving Netsuke in: 1971
Former/Other Occupation(s): Ivory carver (*okimono*)
Main Materials Used: Ivory, mammoth tusk
Favorite Subjects: Human figures
Main Types of Finish: *Yasha* stain

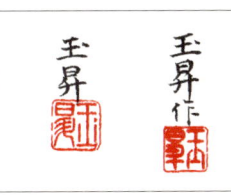

箱書き落款　Signature/seal on the box 　　　銘　Signature

田中治彦　　HARUHIKO Tanaka

本名：田中治彦（1946年生）
出身地：東京都
現住所：山梨県清里の森
根付制作開始：1980年
根付制作以前／以外の仕事：貴金属彫刻
主に使用している材料／材質：金属、宝石
得意とするテーマ：植物、昆虫
主な仕上げ方：無着色

Actual Name: Haruhiko Tanaka (b. 1946)
Place of Birth: Tokyo
Current Address: Yamanashi Prefecture
Began Carving Netsuke in: 1980
Former/Other Occupation(s): Sculptor in precious metals
Main Materials Used: Metal, jewels
Favorite Subjects: Plants, insects
Main Types of Finish: Uncolored

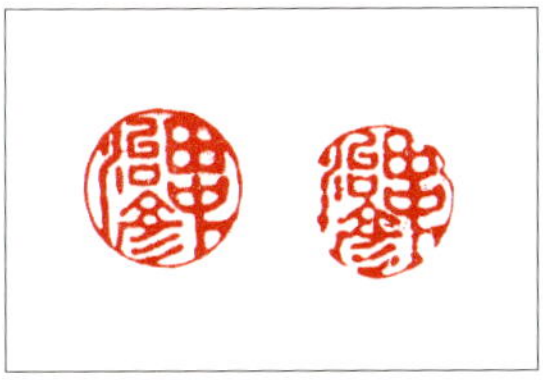

箱書き落款　Signature/seal on the box 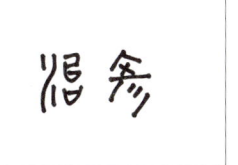　　　銘　Signature

赤木英文　HIDEFUMI Akagi

本名：赤木節夫(1949年生)
出身地：鹿児島県
現住所：鹿児島県大口市
根付制作開始：1974年
根付制作以前／以外の仕事：製版(印刷)
主に使用している材料／材質：象牙、木材
得意とするテーマ：魚介類、小動物
主な仕上げ方：やしゃ染め、染料着色

Actual Name: Setsuo Akagi (b. 1949)
Place of Birth: Kagoshima Prefecture
Current Address: Kagoshima Prefecture
Began Carving Netsuke in: 1974
Former/Other Occupation(s): printer
Main Materials Used: Ivory, wood
Favorite Subjects: Aquatic creatures, small creatures
Main Types of Finish: *Yasha* stain, dyes

箱書き落款　Signature/seal on the box

関沢芳堂　HODO Sekizawa

本名：関沢芳夫(1929年生)
出身地：神奈川県
現住所：神奈川県
根付制作開始：1963年
根付制作以前／以外の仕事：象牙彫刻(置物)
主に使用している材料／材質：象牙
得意とするテーマ：人物
主な仕上げ方：やしゃ染め、漆仕上げ

Actual Name: Yoshio Sekizawa (b. 1929)
Place of Birth: Kanagawa Prefecture
Current Address: Kanagawa Prefecture
Began Carving Netsuke in: 1963
Former/Other Occupation(s): Ivory carver (*okimono*)
Main Materials Used: Ivory
Favorite Subjects: Human figures
Main Types of Finish: *Yasha* stain, lacquer

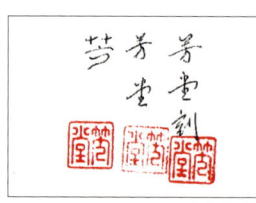

箱書き落款　Signature/seal on the box 　　銘　Signature

宮澤宝泉　HOSEN Miyazawa

本名：宮澤明人(1942年生)
出身地：山梨県
現住所：山梨県西八代郡
根付制作開始：1983年
根付制作以前／以外の仕事：象牙彫刻(置物)
主に使用している材料／材質：象牙、マンモス牙、木材、鹿角、海松
得意とするテーマ：人物、動物、植物
主な仕上げ方：無着色、やしゃ染め、顔料着色、染料着色

Actual Name: Akihito Miyazawa (b. 1942)
Place of Birth: Yamanashi Prefecture
Current Address: Yamanashi Prefecture
Began Carving Netsuke in: 1983
Former/Other Occupation(s): Ivory carver (*okimono*)
Main Materials Used: Ivory, mammoth tusk, wood, stag antler, black coral
Favorite Subjects: Human figures, animals, plants
Main Types of Finish: Uncolored, *yasha* stain, paint, dyes

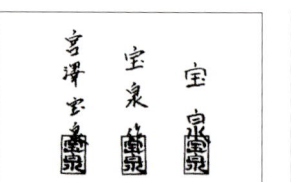

箱書き落款　Signature/seal on the box 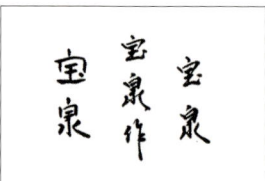　　銘　Signature

山形芳朱　HOSHU Yamagata

本名：山形剛（1932年生）
出身地：東京都
現住所：福島県郡山市
根付制作開始：1947年
主に使用している材料／材質：象牙、木材
得意とするテーマ：人物
主な仕上げ方：無着色、やしゃ染め、顔料（一部染料使用する場合有り）

Actual Name: Tsuyoshi Yamagata (b. 1932)
Place of Birth: Tokyo
Current Address: Fukushima Prefecture
Began Carving Netsuke in: 1947
Main Materials Used: Ivory, wood
Favorite Subjects: Human figures
Main Types of Finish: Uncolored, *yasha* stain, paint (sometimes days)

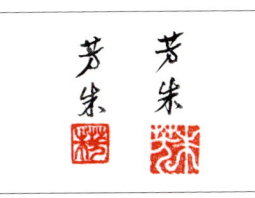

箱書き落款　Signature/seal on the box

銘　Signature

桜井一桜　ICHIO Sakurai

本名：桜井仁郎（1940年～2003年）
根付制作開始：1951年
主に使用している材料／材質：象牙
得意とするテーマ：人物、植物
主な仕上げ方：やしゃ染め、顔料着色

Actual Name: Niro Sakurai (1940-2003)
Began Carving Netsuke in: 1951
Main Materials Used: Ivory
Favorite Subjects: Human figures, plants
Main Types of Finish: *Yasha* stain, paint

銘　Signature

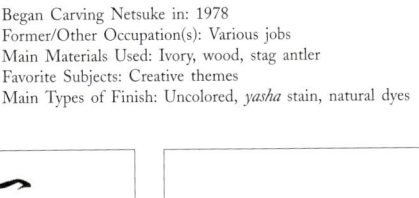

糟谷一空　IKKU Kasuya

本名：糟谷勇（1949年生）
出身地：埼玉県
現住所：埼玉県
根付制作開始：1978年
根付制作以前／以外の仕事：多種類
主に使用している材料／材質：象牙、木材、鹿角
得意とするテーマ：造化
主な仕上げ方：無着色、やしゃ染め、天然染料染め

Actual Name: Isamu Kasuya (b. 1949)
Place of Birth: Saitama Prefecture
Current Address: Saitama Prefecture
Began Carving Netsuke in: 1978
Former/Other Occupation(s): Various jobs
Main Materials Used: Ivory, wood, stag antler
Favorite Subjects: Creative themes
Main Types of Finish: Uncolored, *yasha* stain, natural dyes

箱書き落款　Signature/seal on the box

銘　Signature

安藤五十治　ISOJI Ando

本名：安藤五十治(1956年生)
出身地：石川県
現住所：石川県輪島市
根付制作開始：1986年
根付制作以前／以外の仕事：漆工、蒔絵
主に使用している材料／材質：象牙、木材、鼈甲
得意とするテーマ：植物、天象文
主な仕上げ方：漆

Actual Name: Isoji Ando (b. 1956)
Place of Birth: Ishikawa Prefecture
Current Address: Ishikawa Prefecture
Began Carving Netsuke in: 1986
Former/Other Occupation(s): Lacquer, *maki-e*
Main Materials Used: Ivory, wood, tortoiseshell
Favorite Subjects: Plants, astronomical symbols
Main Types of Finish: Lacquer

箱書き落款　Signature/seal on the box

岸一舟　ISSHU Kishi

本名：岸義雄(1917年生)
出身地：東京都
現住所：埼玉県熊谷市
根付制作開始：1958年
主に使用している材料／材質：象牙
得意とするテーマ：人物
主な仕上げ方：染料着色

Actual Name: Yoshio Kishi (b. 1917)
Place of Birth: Tokyo
Current Address: Saitama Prefecture
Began Carving Netsuke in: 1958
Main Materials Used: Ivory
Favorite Subjects: Human figures
Main Types of Finish: Dyes

箱書き落款　Signature/seal on the box 　　銘　Signature

桑原仁　JIN Kuwabara

本名：桑原宏仁(1956年生)
出身地：群馬県
現住所：埼玉県上尾市
根付制作開始：1997年
根付制作以前／以外の仕事：はく製士
主に使用している材料／材質：象牙
得意とするテーマ：植物、魚介類
主な仕上げ方：染料着色

Actual Name: Koji Kuwabara (b. 1956)
Place of Birth: Gunna Prefecture
Current Address: Saitama Prefecture
Began Carving Netsuke in: 1997
Former/Other Occupation(s): Taxidermist
Main Materials Used: Ivory
Favorite Subjects: Plants, aquatic creatures
Main Types of Finish: Dyes

箱書き落款　Signature/seal on the box 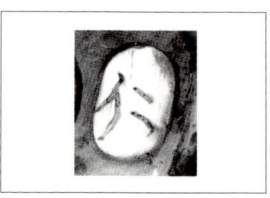　　銘　Signature

梨本寿光　JUKO Nashimoto

本名：梨本義雄（1952年～2005年）
出身地：東京都
現住所：東京都江戸川区
根付制作開始：1978年
根付制作以前／以外の仕事：写真製版
主に使用している材料／材質：象牙
得意とするテーマ：動物
主な仕上げ方：無着色、やしゃ染め、
　染料着色

Actual Name: Nashimoto Yoshio (1952-2005)
Place of Birth: Tokyo
Current Address: Tokyo
Began Carving Netsuke in: 1978
Former/Other Occupation(s): Photographic printing
Main Materials Used: Ivory
Favorite Subjects: Animals
Main Types of Finish: Uncolored, *yasha* stain, dyes

箱書き落款　Signature/seal on the box

小針樹生　JUSHO Kobari

本名：小針直樹（1952年生）
出身地：東京都
現住所：埼玉県さいたま市
根付制作開始：2003年
根付制作以前／以外の仕事：象牙彫刻
主に使用している材料／材質：象牙、木材、鹿
　角
得意とするテーマ：人物
主な仕上げ方：無着色

Actual Name: Naoki Kobari (b. 1952)
Place of Birth: Tokyo
Current Address: Saitama Prefecture
Began Carving Netsuke in: 2003
Former/Other Occupation(s): Ivory carver
Main Materials Used: Ivory, woods, stag antler
Favorite Subjects: Human figures
Main Types of Finish: Uncolored

箱書き落款　Signature/seal on the box 　　銘　Signature

---

立原寛玉　KANGYOKU Tachihara

本名：立原徳彬（1944年生）
出身地：東京都
現住所：埼玉県
根付制作開始：1966年
根付制作以前／以外の仕事：多種類
主に使用している材料／材質：象牙、木材
得意とするテーマ：動物
主な仕上げ方：無着色

Actual Name: Noriyoshi Tachihara (b. 1944)
Place of Birth: Tokyo
Current Address: Saitama Prefecture
Began Carving Netsuke in: 1966
Former/Other Occupation(s): Various jobs
Main Materials Used: Ivory, wood
Favorite Subjects: Animals
Main Types of Finish: Uncolored

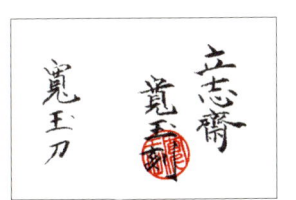

箱書き落款　Signature/seal on the box 　　銘　Signature

蝦名寛弘　　KANKO Ebina

本名：蝦名慶三（1921年～1998年）
出身地：青森県弘前市
現住所：埼玉県戸田
根付制作開始：1980年
根付制作以前／以外の仕事：動物の置物
主に使用している材料／材質：象牙
得意とするテーマ：動物
主な仕上げ方：無着色、やしゃ染め

Actual Name: Keizo Ebina (1921-1998)
Place of Birth: Aomori Prefecture
Current Address: Saitama Prefecture
Began Carving Netsuke in: 1980
Former/Other Occupation(s): Carver (animal figures)
Main Materials Used: Ivory
Favorite Subjects: Animals
Main Types of Finish: Uncolored, *yasha* stain

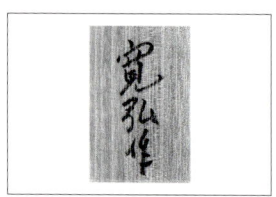

箱書き落款　Signature/seal on the box

若林寛水　　KANSUI Wakabayashi

本名：若林直樹（1955年生）
出身地：岐阜県
現住所：岐阜県
根付制作開始：1985年
根付制作以前／以外の仕事：多種類
主に使用している材料／材質：象牙、木材、鹿角
得意とするテーマ：動物、想像上の動物、霊獣、妖怪
主な仕上げ方：無着色

Actual Name: Naoki Wakabayashi (b. 1955)
Place of Birth: Gifu Prefecture
Current Address: Gifu Prefecture
Began Carving Netsuke in: 1985
Former/Other Occupation(s): Various jobs
Main Materials Used: Ivory, wood, stag antler
Favorite Subjects: Animals, mythical creatures, ghostly beings
Main Types of Finish: Uncolored

箱書き落款　Signature/seal on the box

銘　Signature

水谷一夫　　KAZUO Mizutani

本名：水谷数夫（1932年生）
出身地：東京都
根付制作開始：1947年
主に使用している材料／材質：象牙、木材
得意とするテーマ：動物、植物
主な仕上げ方：やしゃ染め

Actual Name: Kazuo Mizutani (b. 1932)
Place of Birth: Tokyo
Began Carving Netsuke in: 1947
Main Materials Used: Ivory, wood
Favorite Subjects: Animals, plants
Main Types of Finish: *Yasha* stain

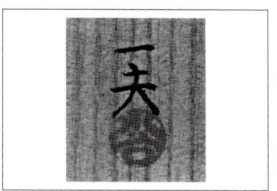

箱書き落款　Signature/seal on the box

阿部賢次　KENJI Abe

本名：阿部賢二（1947年生）
出身地：東京都
現住所：埼玉県
根付制作開始：1983年
根付制作以前／以外の仕事：象牙彫刻（置物）
主に使用している材料／材質：象牙、木材、鹿角、琥珀、堆朱
得意とするテーマ：人物、動物
主な仕上げ方：無着色、やしゃ染め、草木染め

Actual Name: Kenji Abe (b. 1947)
Place of Birth: Tokyo
Current Address: Saitama Prefecture
Began Carving Netsuke in: 1983
Former/Other Occupation(s): Ivory carver (*okimono*)
Main Materials Used: Ivory, wood, stag antler, amber, lacquer
Favorite Subjects: Human figures, animals
Main Types of Finish: Uncolored, *yasha* stain, natural dyes

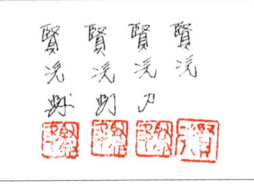

箱書き落款　Signature/seal on the box 　　　銘　Signature

高木喜峰　KIHO Takagi

本名：高木泰喜（1957年生）
出身地：香川県
現住所：香川県
根付制作開始：1992年
根付制作以前／以外の仕事：貴金属加工
主に使用している材料／材質：象牙、マンモス牙、木材、鹿角、海松、金属、琥珀、貝、化石、木の実など
得意とするテーマ：人物、動物、植物、魚介類、物語など
主な仕上げ方：無着色、やしゃ染め、染料着色

Actual Name: Yasuki Takagi (b. 1957)
Place of Birth: Kagawa Prefecture
Current Address: Kagawa Prefecture
Began Carving Netsuke in: 1992
Former/Other Occupation(s): Precious-metal worker
Main Materials Used: Ivory, mammoth tusk, wood, stag antler, black coral, metal, amber, shell, fossils, nuts, etc.
Favorite Subjects: Human figures, animals, plants, aquatic creatures, stories
Main Types of Finish: Uncolored, *yasha* stain, dyes

箱書き落款　Signature/seal on the box 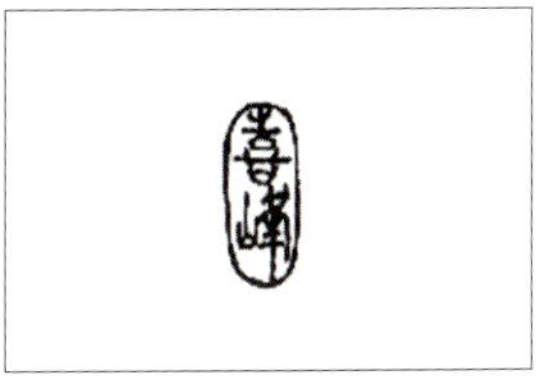　　　銘　Signature

河瀬欽水　KINSUI Kawase

本名：河瀬金一（1926年生）
出身地：三重県
現住所：三重県伊勢市
根付制作開始：1953年頃
根付制作以前／以外の仕事：航空機電気技師
主に使用している材料／材質：木材（黄楊）
得意とするテーマ：人物、動物、植物、魚介類、昆虫類
主な仕上げ方：やしゃ染め、染料着色

Actual Name: Kinichi Kawase (b. 1926)
Place of Birth: Mie Prefecture
Current Address: Mie Prefecture
Began Carving Netsuke in: 1953
Former/Other Occupation(s): Airplane electrical engineer
Main Materials Used: Wood (boxwood)
Favorite Subjects: Human figures, animals, plants, aquatic creatures, insects
Main Types of Finish: *Yasha* stain, dyes

箱書き落款　Signature/seal on the box 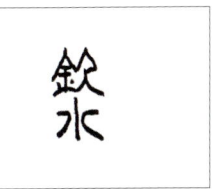　　　銘　Signature

針谷絹代　KINUYO Hariya

本名：針谷絹代（1959年生）
出身地：石川県
現住所：石川県
根付制作開始：1993年
根付制作以前／以外の仕事：漆器蒔絵（茶道具）
主に使用している材料／材質：象牙、木材、琥珀
得意とするテーマ：動物、植物
主な仕上げ方：漆（蒔絵）

Actual Name: Kinuyo Hariya (b. 1959)
Place of Birth: Ishikawa Prefecture
Current Address: Ishikawa Prefecture
Began Carving Netsuke in: 1993
Former/Other Occupation(s): Lacquer (*maki-e*) artist (tea-ceremony utensils)
Main Materials Used: Ivory, wood, amber
Favorite Subjects: Animals, plants
Main Types of Finish: Lacquer (*maki-e*)

箱書き落款　Signature/seal on the box 　　銘　Signature

大下香仙　KOSEN Oshita

本名：大下元行（1948年生）
出身地：石川県
現住所：石川県加賀市
根付制作開始：1978年
根付制作以前／以外の仕事：漆芸蒔絵（茶道具）
主に使用している材料／材質：象牙、木材
得意とするテーマ：植物
主な仕上げ方：漆、蒔絵

Actual Name: Motoyuki Oshita (b. 1948)
Place of Birth: Ishikawa Prefecture
Current Address: Ishikawa Prefecture
Began Carving Netsuke in: 1978
Former/Other Occupation(s): Lacquer (*maki-e*) artist (tea-ceremony utensils)
Main Materials Used: Ivory, wood
Favorite Subjects: Plants
Main Types of Finish: Lacquer, *maki-e*

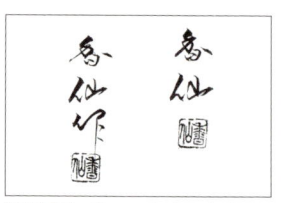

箱書き落款　Signature/seal on the box

福山恒山　KOZAN Fukuyama

本名：福山恒夫（1946年生）
出身地：愛媛県
現住所：愛媛県
根付制作開始：1987年
根付制作以前／以外の仕事：多種類
主に使用している材料／材質：象牙、木材、鹿角、海松
得意とするテーマ：動物、河童
主な仕上げ方：無着色、やしゃ染め、顔料着色、染料着色

Actual Name: Tsuneo Fukuyama (b. 1946)
Place of Birth: Ehime Prefecture
Current Address: Ehime Prefecture
Began Carving Netsuke in: 1987
Former/Other Occupation(s): Various jobs
Main Materials Used: Ivory, wood, stag antler, black coral
Favorite Subjects: Animals, *kappa* (water sprites)
Main Types of Finish: Uncolored, *yasha* stain, paint, dyes

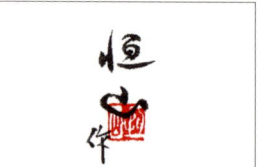

箱書き落款　Signature/seal on the box 　　銘　Signature

中村空哉　KUYA Nakamura

本名：さはら慎三、後に中村慎三（1881年～1961年）
出身地：東京都
根付制作期間：1920年～1961年
根付制作以前／以外の仕事：象牙彫刻（置物）
主に使用している材料／材質：象牙、黄楊
得意とするテーマ：仏教主題
主な仕上げ方：無着色、やしゃ染め

Actual Name: Takakazu (Shinzo) Sahara, later Shinzo Nakamura (1881-1961)
Place of Birth: Tokyo
Carved Netsuke in: 1920-1961
Former/Other Occupation(s): Ivory carver (*okimono*)
Main Materials Used: Ivory, boxwood
Favorite Subjects: Buddhist subjects
Main Types of Finish: Uncolored, *yasha* stain

銘　Signature

斎藤昌寛　MASAHIRO Saito

本名：斎藤昌寛（1970年生）
出身地：埼玉県
現住所：埼玉県
主に使用している材料／材質：象牙、木材、鹿角
得意とするテーマ：動物、魚介類
主な仕上げ方：やしゃ染め、顔料着色、染料着色、漆

Actual Name: Masahiro Saito (b. 1970)
Place of Birth: Saitama Prefecture
Current Address: Saitama Prefecture
Main Materials Used: Ivory, wood, stag antler
Favorite Subjects: Animals, aquatic creatures
Main Types of Finish: *Yasha* stain, paint, dyes, lacquer

箱書き落款　Signature/seal on the box

阪井正美　MASAMI Sakai

本名：阪井美代（1937年生）
出身地：三重県
現住所：三重県
根付制作開始：1973年
根付制作以前／以外の仕事：主婦
主に使用している材料／材質：木材、海松
得意とするテーマ：動物
主な仕上げ方：染料着色

Actual Name: Miyo Sakai (b. 1937)
Place of Birth: Mie Prefecture
Current Address: Mie Prefecture
Began Carving Netsuke in: 1973
Former/Other Occupation(s): Housewife
Main Materials Used: Wood, black coral
Favorite Subjects: Animals
Main Types of Finish: Dyes

箱書き落款　Signature/seal on the box 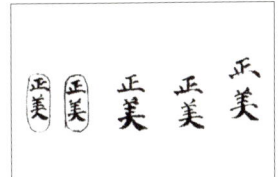　　　銘　Signature

中村雅俊　MASATOSHI Nakamura

本名：中村時定(1915年〜2001年)
出身地：東京都
根付制作期間：1939年〜2001年
主に使用している材料／材質：象牙、マンモス牙、木材、鹿角、海松、犀角、琥珀、鯨歯、河馬の歯
得意とするテーマ：人物、動物、魚介類、化け物、空想の物
主な仕上げ方：無着色、やしゃ染め、漆、カリウム重クローム酸、クチナシ

Actual Name: Tokisada Nakamura (1915-2001)
Place of Birth: Tokyo
Carved Netsuke in: 1939-2001
Main Materials Used: Ivory, mammoth tusk, wood, stag antler, black coral, rhinoceros horn, amber, whale tooth, hippopotamus tooth
Favorite Subjects: Human figures, animals, aquatic creatures, imaginary beings
Main Types of Finish: Uncolored, *yasha* stain, lacquer, potassium bichromate, gardenia stain

箱書き落款　Signature/seal on the box 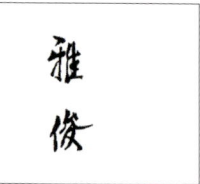　　銘　Signature

針谷祐之　MASAYUKI Hariya

本名：針谷祐之(1954年生)
出身地：石川県
現住所：石川県江沼郡
根付制作開始：1993年
根付制作以前／以外の仕事：漆器蒔絵(茶道具)
主に使用している材料／材質：象牙、木材、琥珀
得意とするテーマ：動物、植物、魚介類
主な仕上げ方：漆(蒔絵)

Actual Name: Masayuki Hariya (b. 1954)
Place of Birth: Ishikawa Prefecture
Current Address: Ishikawa Prefecture
Began Carving Netsuke in: 1993
Former/Other Occupation(s): Lacquer (*maki-e*) artist (tea ceremony utensils)
Main Materials Used: Ivory, wood, amber
Favorite Subjects: Animals, plants, aquatic creatures
Main Types of Finish: Lacquer (*maki-e*)

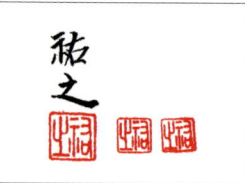

箱書き落款　Signature/seal on the box 　　銘　Signature

森田正行　MASAYUKI Morita

本名：森田正行(1952年生)
出身地：岩手県
現住所：石川県
根付制作開始：1985年
根付制作以前／以外の仕事：木彫刻
主に使用している材料／材質：木材
得意とするテーマ：動物、虫類
主な仕上げ方：無着色、やしゃ染め、顔料着色、染料着色、漆

Actual Name: Masayuki Morita (b. 1952)
Place of Birth: Iwate Prefecture
Current Address: Ishikawa Prefecture
Began Carving Netsuke in: 1985
Former/Other Occupation(s): Wood carver
Main Materials Used: wood
Favorite Subjects: Animals, insects
Main Types of Finish: Uncolored, *yasha* stain, paint, dyes, lacquer

箱書き落款　Signature/seal on the box

平賀明玉斎　　MEIGYOKUSAI Hiraga

本名：平賀胤次（1896年～1991年）
出身地：東京都
根付制作期間：1970年代～1991年
根付制作以前／以外の仕事：象牙彫刻（置物）
主に使用している材料／材質：象牙
得意とするテーマ：人物、動物
主な仕上げ方：やしゃ染め

Actual Name: Tanetsugu Hiraga (1896-1991)
Place of Birth: Tokyo
Carved Netsuke in: 1970-1991
Former/Other Occupation(s): Ivory carver (*okimono*)
Main Materials Used: Ivory
Favorite Subjects: Human figures, animals
Main Types of Finish: *Yasha* stain

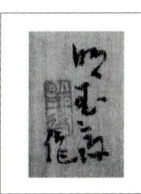

箱書き落款　Signature/seal on the box 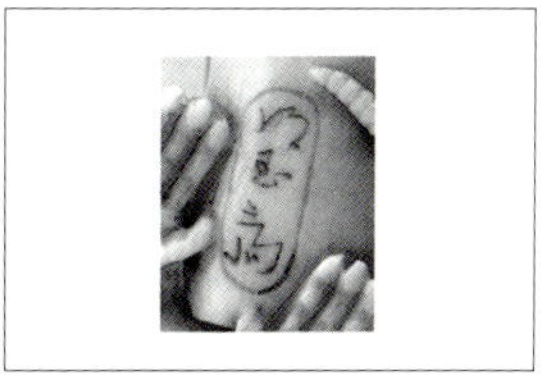　　銘　Signature

---

庄司明幹　　MEIKAN Shoji

本名：庄司富雄（1936年生）
出身地：山形県
現住所：東京都足立区
根付制作開始：1974年
根付制作以前／以外の仕事：象牙アクセサリー
　　彫刻
主に使用している材料／材質：象牙、マンモス
　　牙、木材、鹿角
得意とするテーマ：人物、動物、植
　　物
主な仕上げ方：無着色、やしゃ染め、
　　顔料着色、染料着色、漆

Actual Name: Tomio Shoji (b. 1936)
Place of Birth: Yamagata Prefecture
Current Address: Tokyo
Began Carving Netsuke in: 1974
Former/Other Occupation(s): Ivory ornament carver
Main Materials Used: Ivory, mammoth tusk, wood, stag antler
Favorite Subjects: Human figures, animals, plants
Main Types of Finish: Uncolored, *yasha* stain, paint, dyes, lacquer

箱書き落款　Signature/seal on the box 　　銘　Signature

---

河原明秀　　MEISHU (AKIHIDE) Kawahara

本名：河原明（1934年生）
出身地：東京都
現住所：埼玉県朝霞市
根付制作開始：1958年
根付制作以前／以外の仕事：象牙彫刻
主に使用している材料／材質：象牙、木材、鹿
　　角
得意とするテーマ：人物、動物
主な仕上げ方：無着色、やしゃ染め

Actual Name: Akira Kawahara (b. 1934)
Place of Birth: Tokyo
Current Address: Saitama Prefecture
Began Carving Netsuke in: 1958
Former/Other Occupation(s): Ivory carver
Main Materials Used: Ivory, wood, stag antler
Favorite Subjects: Human figures, animals
Main Types of Finish: Uncolored, *yasha* stain

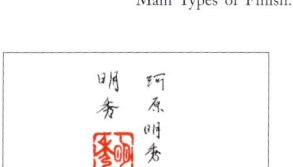

箱書き落款　Signature/seal on the box 　　銘　Signature

篠崎藍青　　RANJO Shinozaki

本名：篠崎松男（1946年生）
出身地：東京都中野区
現住所：千葉県野田市
根付制作開始：1977年
根付制作以前／以外の仕事：多種類
主に使用している材料／材質：象牙、木材
得意とするテーマ：動物
主な仕上げ方：無着色、やしゃ染め

Actual Name: Matsuo Shinozaki (b. 1946)
Place of Birth: Tokyo
Current Address: Chiba Prefecture
Began Carving Netsuke in: 1977
Former/Other Occupation(s): Various jobs
Main Materials Used: Ivory, wood
Favorite Subjects: Animals
Main Types of Finish: Uncolored, *yasha* stain

箱書き落款　Signature/seal on the box	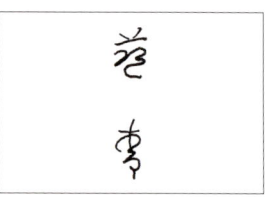 銘　Signature

矢部梁生　　RYOSEI Yabe

本名：矢部勇（1932年生）
出身地：埼玉県
現住所：埼玉県
根付制作開始：1968年
根付制作以前／以外の仕事：象牙彫刻（置物）
主に使用している材料／材質：象牙
得意とするテーマ：人物
主な仕上げ方：やしゃ染め、顔料着
　　　　　　　色、漆

Actual Name: Isamu Yabe (b. 1932)
Place of Birth: Saitama Prefecture
Current Address: Saitama Prefecture
Began Carving Netsuke in: 1968
Former/Other Occupation(s): Ivory carver (*okimono*)
Main Materials Used: Ivory
Favorite Subjects: Human figures
Main Types of Finish: *Yasha* stain, paint, lacquer

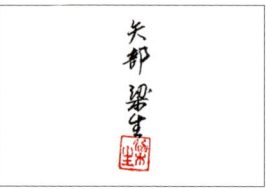

箱書き落款　Signature/seal on the box	 銘　Signature

秋田綾泉　　RYOSEN Akita

本名：秋田政宏（1932年生）
出身地：東京都
現住所：東京都葛飾区
根付制作開始：1982年
根付制作以前／以外の仕事：象牙人物置物彫刻
主に使用している材料／材質：象牙、マンモス
得意とするテーマ：人物
主な仕上げ方：やしゃ染め

Actual Name: Masahiro Akita (b. 1932)
Place of Birth: Tokyo
Current Address: Tokyo
Began Carving Netsuke in: 1982
Former/Other Occupation(s): Ivory carver (*okimono*)
Main Materials Used: Ivory, mammoth tusk
Favorite Subjects: Human figures
Main Types of Finish: *Yasha* stain

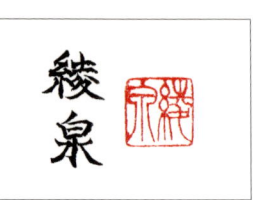

箱書き落款　Signature/seal on the box

宮澤良舟（二代）　RYOSHU Miyazawa II

本名：宮澤正蔵(1912年～1982年)
出身地：東京都
根付制作期間：1927年～1982年
根付制作以前／以外の仕事：象牙彫刻（置物）
主に使用している材料／材質：象牙
得意とするテーマ：動物、植物、魚介類、河童
主な仕上げ方：無着色、やしゃ染め、墨仕上げ

Actual Name: Shozo Miyazawa (1912-82)
Place of Birth: Tokyo
Carved Netsuke in: 1927-1982
Former/Other Occupation(s): Ivory carver (*okimono*)
Main Materials Used: Ivory
Favorite Subjects: Animals, plants, aquatic creatures, *kappa* (water sprites)
Main Types of Finish: Uncolored, *yasha* stain, India ink

箱書き落款　Signature/seal on the box 　　　銘　Signature

---

宮澤良舟（三代）　RYOSHU Miyazawa III

本名：宮澤正太郎(1949年生)
出身地：東京都
現住所：東京都荒川区
根付制作開始：1973年
主に使用している材料／材質：象牙
得意とするテーマ：動物、魚介類、鳥
主な仕上げ方：無着色、やしゃ染め、顔料着色

Actual Name: Shotaro Miyazawa (b. 1949)
Place of Birth: Tokyo
Current Address: Tokyo
Began Carving Netsuke in: 1973
Main Materials Used: Ivory
Favorite Subjects: Animals, aquatic creatures, birds
Main Types of Finish: Uncolored, *yasha* stain, paint

箱書き落款　Signature/seal on the box 　　　銘　Signature

---

椿井龍　RYU Tsubai

本名：椿井克巳(1957年生)
出身地：千葉県
現住所：千葉県千葉市
根付制作開始：1994年
根付制作以前／以外の仕事：グラフィックデザイナー、指圧
主に使用している材料／材質：象牙、マンモス牙、木材、鹿角、海松、金属
得意とするテーマ：人物、動物、植物、魚介類、怪異
主な仕上げ方：無着色、やしゃ染め、顔料着色、染料着色、漆

Actual Name: Katsumi Tsubai (b. 1957)
Place of Birth: Chiba Prefecture
Current Address: Chiba Prefecture
Began Carving Netsuke in: 1994
Former/Other Occupation(s): Graphic designer, shiatsu
Main Materials Used: Ivory, mammoth tusk, wood, stag antler, black coral, metal
Favorite Subjects: Human figures, animals, plants, aquatic creatures, monsters
Main Types of Finish: Uncolored, *yasha* stain, paint, dyes, lacquer

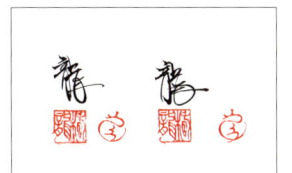

箱書き落款　Signature/seal on the box 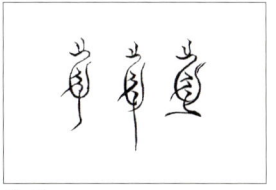　　　銘　Signature

駒田柳之　　RYUSHI Komada

本名：駒田勇（1934年生）
出身地：東京都
現住所：千葉県東葛飾郡
根付制作開始：1970年
根付制作以前／以外の仕事：象牙彫刻（置物）
主に使用している材料／質：象牙、マンモス
　　牙、木材、鹿角、海松
得意とするテーマ：人物
主な仕上げ方：無着色、やしゃ染め、
　　顔料着色

Actual Name: Isamu Komada (b. 1934)
Place of Birth: Tokyo
Current Address: Chiba Prefecture
Began Carving Netsuke in: 1970
Former/Other Occupation(s): Ivory carver (*okimono*)
Main Materials Used: Ivory, mammoth tusk, wood, stag antler, black coral
Favorite Subjects: Human figures
Main Types of Finish: Uncolored, *yasha* stain, paint

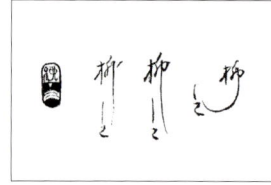

箱書き落款　Signature/seal on the box　　　銘　Signature

寄金佐和子　　SAWAKO Yorikane

本名：寄金佐和子（1962年生）
出身地：東京都
現住所：東京都
根付制作期間：1985年～1995年
主に使用している材料／質：象牙、木
主な仕上げ方：やしゃ染め、染料着色

Actual Name: Sawako Yorikane (b. 1962)
Place of Birth: Tokyo
Current Address: Tokyo
Carved Netsuke in: 1985-1995
Main Materials Used: Ivory, wood
Main Types of Finish: *Yasha* stain, dyes

箱書き落款　Signature/seal on the box

東声方　　SEIHO Azuma

本名：東勝男（1937年～2003年）
出身地：茨城県
根付制作期間：1983年～2003年
根付制作以前／以外の仕事：象牙彫刻（置物）
主に使用している材料／質：象牙、マンモス
　　牙、木材
得意とするテーマ：人物
主な仕上げ方：無着色、やしゃ染め

Actual Name: Katsuo Azuma (1937-2003)
Place of Birth: Ibaraki Prefecture
Carved Netsuke in: 1983-2003
Former/Other Occupation(s): Ivory carver (*okimono*)
Main Materials Used: Ivory, mammoth tusk, wood
Favorite Subjects: Human figures
Main Types of Finish: Uncolored, *yasha* stain

箱書き落款　Signature/seal on the box　　　銘　Signature

高山清水　SEISUI Takayama

本名：高山清一(1949年生)
出身地：三重県多気郡
現住所：三重県多気郡
根付制作期間：1975年
根付制作以前／以外の仕事：学習塾(自営)
主に使用している材料／材質：木材、鹿角、動物の牙
得意とするテーマ：人物、動物、植物、魚介類
主な仕上げ方：無着色、やしゃ染め、染料着色

Actual Name: Seiichi Takayama (b. 1949)
Place of Birth: Mie Prefecture
Current Address: Mie Prefecture
Began Carving Netsuke in: 1975
Former/Other Occupation(s): Private cram school
Main Materials Used: Wood, stag antler, tusks
Favorite Subjects: Human figures, animals, plants, aquatic creatures
Main Types of Finish: Uncolored, *yasha* stain, dyes

箱書き落款　Signature/seal on the box 　　銘　Signature

小林仙歩　SENPO Kobayashi

本名：小林千吉(1919年～1994年)
出身地：東京都
根付制作期間：1954年～1994年
根付制作以前／以外の仕事：象牙彫刻
主に使用している材料／材質：象牙、マンモス牙、木材
得意とするテーマ：動物、昆虫、蛙
主な仕上げ方：無着色、やしゃ染め

Actual Name: Senkichi Kobayashi (1919-1994)
Place of Birth: Tokyo
Carved Netsuke in: 1954-1994
Former/Other Occupation(s): Ivory carver
Main Materials Used: Ivory, mammoth tusk, wood
Favorite Subjects: Animals, insects, frogs
Main Types of Finish: Uncolored, *yasha* stain

箱書き落款　Signature/seal on the box 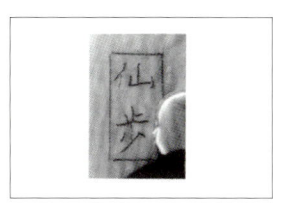　　銘　Signature

村松親月　SHINGETSU Muramatsu

本名：村松藤男(1934年生)
出身地：東京都
現住所：群馬県
根付制作開始：1983年
根付制作以前／以外の仕事：象牙彫刻(置物)
主に使用している材料／材質：象牙
得意とするテーマ：鳥
主な仕上げ方：染料着色

Actual Name: Fujio Muramatsu (b. 1934)
Place of Birth: Tokyo
Current Address: Gunma Prefecture
Began Carving Netsuke in: 1934
Former/Other Occupation(s): Ivory carver (*okimono*)
Main Materials Used: Ivory
Favorite Subjects: Birds
Main Types of Finish: Dyes

箱書き落款　Signature/seal on the box 　　銘　Signature

柳瀬新一郎　SHINICHIRO Yanase

本名：柳瀬新一郎(1969年生)
出身地：東京都
現住所：埼玉県
根付制作開始：1989年
根付制作以前／以外の仕事：一位一刀彫り
主に使用している材料／材質：象牙、木材
得意とするテーマ：動物
主な仕上げ方：蠟びき

Actual Name: Shinichiro Yanase (b. 1969)
Place of Birth: Tokyo
Current Address: Saitama Prefecture
Began Carving Netsuke in: 1989
Former/Other Occupation(s): Wood carver
Main Materials Used: Ivory, wood (yew)
Favorite Subjects: Animals
Main Types of Finish: Beeswax

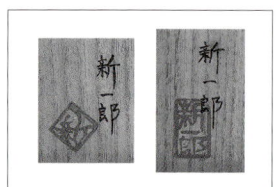

箱書き落款　Signature/seal on the box

鈴木親良　SHINRYO Suzuki

本名：鈴木良三(1910年～1989年)
出身地：東京都
根付制作期間：1948年～1982年
根付制作以前／以外の仕事：象牙彫刻
主に使用している材料／材質：象牙
得意とするテーマ：動物、人物
主な仕上げ方：やしゃ染め、顔料着色

Actual Name: Ryozo Suzuki (1910-1989)
Place of Birth: Tokyo
Carved Netsuke in: 1948-1982
Former/Other Occupation(s): Ivory carver
Main Materials Used: Ivory
Favorite Subjects: Animals, human figures
Main Types of Finish: *Yasha* stain, paint

箱書き落款　Signature/seal on the box 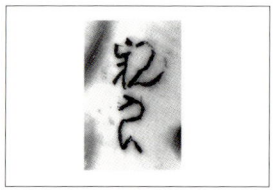　　銘　Signature

一川信山　SHINZAN Ichikawa

本名：一川信吉(1948年生)
出身地：群馬県
現住所：埼玉県越谷市
根付制作開始：1968年
主に使用している材料／材質：象牙
得意とするテーマ：人物、動物
主な仕上げ方：やしゃ染め

Actual Name: Shinkichi Ichikawa (b. 1948)
Place of Birth: Gunma Prefecture
Current Address: Saitama Prefecture
Began Carving Netsuke in: 1968
Main Materials Used: Ivory
Favorite Subjects: Human figures, animals
Main Types of Finish: *Yasha* stain

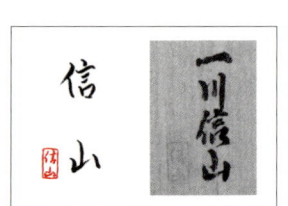

箱書き落款　Signature/seal on the box 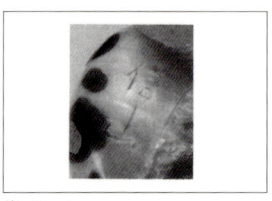　　銘　Signature

木村静　　SHIZUKA Kimura

本名：木村静（1942年生）
出身地：埼玉県
現住所：埼玉県
根付制作開始：1991年
根付制作以前／以外の仕事：会社員
主に使用している材料／材質：象牙、木材
得意とするテーマ：動物、植物
主な仕上げ方：やしゃ染め、染料着色

Actual Name: Shizuka Kimura (b. 1942)
Place of Birth: Saitama Prefecture
Current Address: Saitama Prefecture
Began Carving Netsuke in: 1991
Former/Other Occupation(s): Office worker
Main Materials Used: Ivory, wood
Favorite Subjects: Animals, plants
Main Types of Finish: *Yasha* stain, dyes

箱書き落款　Signature/seal on the box 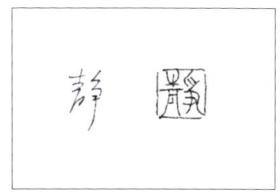　　　銘　Signature

天野松月　　SHOGETSU Amano

本名：天野喜久雄（1887年～1980年）
出身地：千葉県
根付制作期間：1930年～1979年
主に使用している材料／材質：象牙
得意とするテーマ：人物
主な仕上げ方：やしゃ染め

Actual Name: Kikuo Amano (1887-1980)
Place of Birth: Chiba Prefecture
Carved Netsuke in: 1930-1979
Main Materials Used: Ivory
Favorite Subjects: Human figures
Main Types of Finish: *Yasha* stain

箱書き落款　Signature/seal on the box 　　　銘　Signature

西野昇己　　SHOKO Nishino

本名：西野昇太郎（1915年～1972年）
出身地：東京都
根付制作期間：1930年～1969年
主に使用している材料／材質：黄楊
得意とするテーマ：仏教主題
主な仕上げ方：染料着色

Actual Name: Shotaro Nishino (1915-1972)
Place of Birth: Tokyo
Carved Netsuke in: 1930-1969
Main Materials Used: Boxwood
Favorite Subjects: Buddhist subjects
Main Types of Finish: Dyes

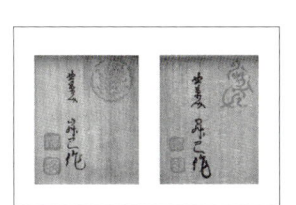

箱書き落款　Signature/seal on the box 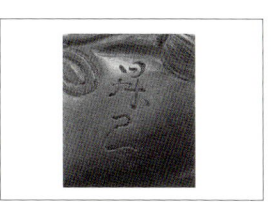　　　銘　Signature

八川秀方　SHUHO Yagawa

本名：八川道雄（1919年生）
出身地：埼玉県
根付制作期間：1942年〜1996年
根付制作以前／以外の仕事：象牙彫刻（置物）
主に使用している材料／材質：象牙
得意とするテーマ：花、柿、果物類、きのこ
主な仕上げ方：無着色、やしゃ染め、染料着色

Actual Name: Michio Yagawa (b. 1919)
Place of Birth: Saitama Prefecture
Carved Netsuke in: 1942-1996
Former/Other Occupation(s): Ivory carver (*okimono*)
Main Materials Used: Ivory
Favorite Subjects: Flowers, persimmons, fruit, mushrooms
Main Types of Finish: Uncolored, *yasha* stain, dyes

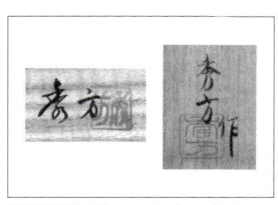

箱書き落款　Signature/seal on the box 　　銘　Signature

大内藻水　SOSUI Ouchi

本名：大内次郎（1911年〜1972年）
出身地：東京都
根付制作期間：1923年〜1972年
主に使用している材料／材質：黄楊
得意とするテーマ：特に人物（歌舞伎、浮世絵も題材とした）
主な仕上げ方：やしゃ染め

Actual Name: Jiro Ouchi (1911-1972)
Place of Birth: Tokyo
Carved Netsuke in: 1923-1972
Main Materials Used: Boxwood
Favorite Subjects: Particularly human figures (including Kabuki and *ukiyo-e* themes)
Main Types of Finish: *Yasha* stain

箱書き落款　Signature/seal on the box 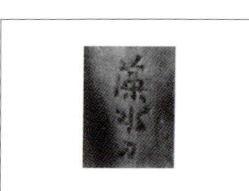　　銘　Signature

佐田澄（寿美）　SUMI Sata

本名：佐田澄子（1944年生）
出身地：兵庫県
現住所：千葉県
根付制作開始：1978年
主に使用している材料／材質：象牙
得意とするテーマ：人物、動物（猫）、人魚、河童
主な仕上げ方：無着色

Actual Name: Sumiko Sata (b. 1944)
Place of Birth: Hyogo Prefecture
Current Address: Chiba Prefecture
Began Carving Netsuke in: 1978
Main Materials Used: Ivory
Favorite Subjects: Human figures, animals (cats), mermaids, *kappa* (water sprites)
Main Types of Finish: Uncolored

箱書き落款　Signature/seal on the box 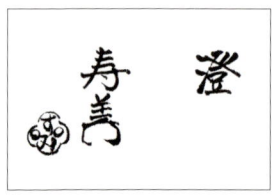　　銘　Signature

弓削忠仙　　TADAHISA (SACHIKO) Yuge

本名：弓削祥子（1947年生）
出身地：岐阜県
現住所：三重県
根付制作開始：1994年
根付制作以前／以外の仕事：漆芸
主に使用している材料／材質：木材
得意とするテーマ：植物、魚介類
主な仕上げ方：無着色、染料着色、
　　　　　　　漆

Actual Name: Sachiko Yuge (b. 1947)
Place of Birth: Gifu Prefecture
Current Address: Mie Prefecture
Began Carving Netsuke in: 1994
Former/Other Occupation(s): Lacquer artist
Main Materials Used: Wood
Favorite Subjects: Plants, aquatic creatures
Main Types of Finish: Uncolored, dyes, lacquer

箱書き落款　Signature/seal on the box 　　銘　Signature

中川忠雲　　TADAKUMO Nakagawa

本名：大西弘祐（1969年生）
出身地：奈良県
現住所：京都府
根付制作開始：1994年
根付制作以前／以外の仕事：ファッションデザ
　　　　　　　　　　　　　　イン
主に使用している材料／材質：木材（主に黄楊）
得意とするテーマ：動物
主な仕上げ方：やしゃ染め、茶粉

Actual Name: Kosuke Onishi (b. 1969)
Place of Birth: Nara Prefecture
Current Address: Kyoto Prefecture
Began Carving Netsuke in: 1994
Former/Other Occupation(s): Fashion designer
Main Materials Used: Wood (esp. boxwood)
Favorite Subjects: Animals
Main Types of Finish: *Yasha* stain, powdered tea

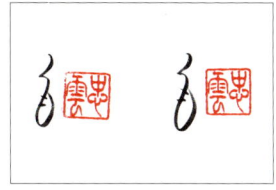

箱書き落款　Signature/seal on the box

中川忠峰　　TADAMINE Nakagawa

本名：中川俊夫（1947年生）
出身地：三重県
現住所：三重県伊勢市
根付制作開始：1980年
根付制作以前／以外の仕事：木工、木彫
主に使用している材料／材質：木材（主に黄楊）
得意とするテーマ：人物、動物、植物、魚介類
主な仕上げ方：やしゃ染め、染料着
　　　　　　　色

Actual Name: Toshio Nakagawa (b. 1947)
Place of Birth: Mie Prefecture
Current Address: Mie Prefecture
Began Carving Netsuke in: 1980
Former/Other Occupation(s): Carpenter, sculptor (wood)
Main Materials Used: Wood (esp. boxwood)
Favorite Subjects: Human figures, animals, plants, aquatic
　　creatures
Main Types of Finish: *Yasha* stain, dyes

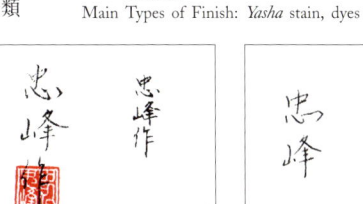

箱書き落款　Signature/seal on the box 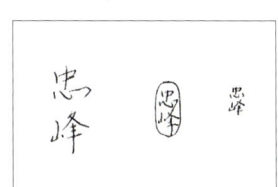　　銘　Signature

北村隆　TAKASHI Kitamura

本名：北村隆（1946年生）
出身地：石川県
現住所：石川県小松市
根付制作期間：1996年に3点を特別制作
根付制作以前／以外の仕事：陶芸家
主に使用している材料／材質：陶磁器
得意とするテーマ：人物、動物、植物、魚介類
主な仕上げ方：九谷焼、伝統古九谷焼風、金彩、
　　錦絵風

Actual Name: Takashi Kitamura (b. 1946)
Place of Birth: Ishikawa Prefecture
Current Address: Ishikawa Prefecture
Made Netsuke in: 1996 (3 pieces)
Former/Other Occupation(s): Ceramics
Main Materials Used: Ceramics, porcelain
Favorite Subjects: Human figures, animals, plants, aquatic creatures
Main Types of Finish: Kutani, traditional Ko-Kutani style, *kinsai*, *nishiki-e* style

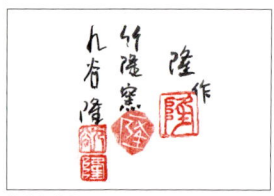

箱書き落款　Signature/seal on the box

中村多美　TAMI Nakamura

本名：中村多美（1946年～2001年）
出身地：東京都
根付制作開始：1992年
根付制作以前／以外の仕事：主婦
主に使用している材料／材質：象牙、木材
得意とするテーマ：動物
主な仕上げ方：やしゃ染め

Actual Name: Tami Nakamura (1946-2001)
Place of Birth: Tokyo
Began Carving Netsuke in: 1992
Former/Other Occupation(s): housewife
Main Materials Used: Ivory, wood
Favorite Subjects: Animals
Main Types of Finish: *Yasha* stain

箱書き落款　Signature/seal on the box

平賀胤寿　TANETOSHI Hiraga

本名：平賀胤壽（1947年生）
出身地：京都府
現住所：滋賀県
根付制作開始：1973年
根付制作以前／以外の仕事：象牙彫刻（置物）
主に使用している材料／材質：象牙、木材
得意とするテーマ：人物、動物、髑髏
主な仕上げ方：やしゃ染め、顔料着
　　色

Actual Name: Tanetoshi Hiraga (b. 1947)
Place of Birth: Kyoto Prefecture
Current Address: Shiga Prefecture
Began Carving Netsuke in: 1973
Former/Other Occupation(s): Ivory carver (*okimono*)
Main Materials Used: Ivory, wood
Favorite Subjects: Human figures, animals, skulls
Main Types of Finish: *Yasha* stain, paint

箱書き落款　Signature/seal on the box 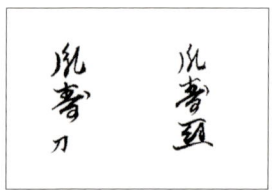　　　銘　Signature

森哲郎　　TETSURO Mori

本名：森哲郎（1960年生）
出身地：東京都
現住所：神奈川県藤沢市
根付制作開始：1995年
根付制作以前／以外の仕事：電気工事
主に使用している材料／材質：象牙、マンモス牙、木材、鹿角
得意とするテーマ：人物、植物
主な仕上げ方：無着色、やしゃ染め、草木染め

Actual Name: Tetsuro Mori (b. 1960)
Place of Birth: Tokyo
Current Address: Kanagawa Prefecture
Began Carving Netsuke in: 1995
Former/Other Occupation(s): Electrician
Main Materials Used: Ivory, mammoth tusk, wood, stag antler
Favorite Subjects: Human figures, plants
Main Types of Finish: Uncolored, *yasha* stain, natural dyes

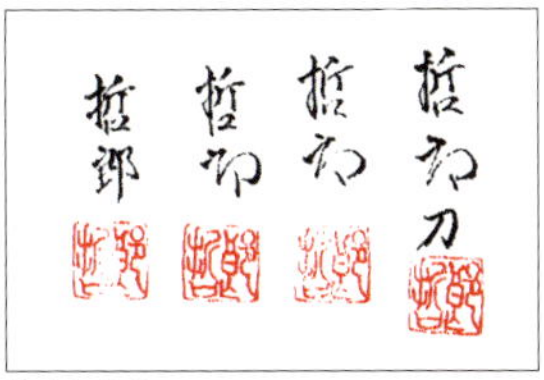

箱書き落款　Signature/seal on the box 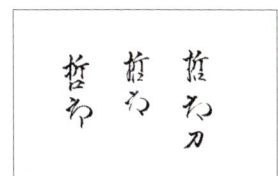　　銘　Signature

---

中村富栄　　TOMIE Nakamura

本名：中村富栄（1925年～1993年）
出身地：東京都
根付制作期間：1993年に2点を特別制作
根付制作以外の仕事：漆芸家、クラフト・センター・ジャパン（財）理事、日本クラフトデザイン協会理事
主に使用している材料／材質：堆朱

Actual Name: Tomie Nakamura (1925-1993)
Place of Birth: Tokyo
Carved Netsuke in: 1993 (carved 2 pieces)
Other Occupation(s): Lacquer artist; Director, Craft Center Japan; Director, Japan Craft Design Association
Main Materials Used: *Tsuishu* lacquer

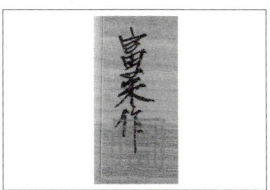

箱書き落款　Signature/seal on the box

更谷富造　　TOMIZO Saratani

本名：更谷富造（1949年生）
出身地：京都府
現住所：北海道上川郡
根付制作開始：1994年（緒締、1985年）
根付制作以前の仕事：漆工芸家
主に使用している材料／材質：象牙、木、海松、漆
得意とするテーマ：動物、植物、昆虫類
主な仕上げ方：漆

Actual Name: Tomizo Saratani (b. 1949)
Place of Birth: Kyoto Prefecture
Current Address: Hokkaido Prefecture
Began Carving Netsuke in: 1994 (*ojime* from 1985)
Former Occupation: Lacquer artist
Main Materials Used: Ivory, wood, black coral, lacquer
Favorite Subjects: Animals, plants, insects
Main Types of Finish: Lacquer

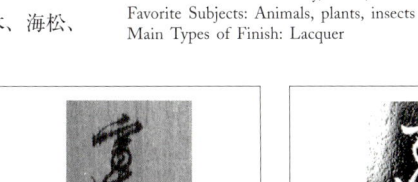

箱書き落款　Signature/seal on the box 　　銘　Signature

田中俊晞　TOSHIKI Tanaka

本名：田中俊晞（1942年生）
出身地：島根県
現住所：江津市嘉久町
根付制作開始：1973年
根付制作以前／以外の仕事：会社員・彫刻家
主に使用している材料／材質：木材、海松、猪牙、カバの歯
得意とするテーマ：小動物、魚介類
　（2004年島根県ふるさと伝統工芸品「石見根付」指定）
主な仕上げ方：無着色、やしゃ染め

Actual Name: Toshiki Tanaka (b. 1942)
Place of Birth: Shimane Prefecture
Current Address: Shimane Prefecture
Began Carving Netsuke in: 1973
Former/Other Occupation(s): Office worker, sculptor
Main Materials Used: Wood, black coral, boar tusk, hippopotamus tooth
Favorite Subjects: Small creatures, aquatic creatures
Main Types of Finish: Uncolored, *yasha* stain

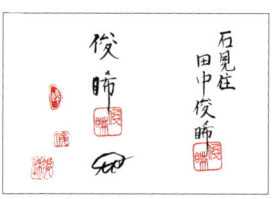

箱書き落款　Signature/seal on the box 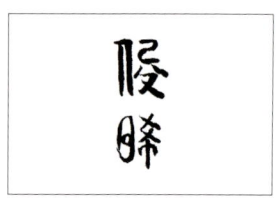　　銘　Signature

---

宍戸濤雲　TOUN Shishido

本名：宍戸濤一（1960年生）
出身地：千葉県
現住所：埼玉県さいたま市
根付制作開始：1997年
根付制作以前／以外の仕事：貴金属加工
主に使用している材料／材質：象牙、マンモス、木材、金属、琥珀
得意とするテーマ：動物、植物、魚介類
主な仕上げ方：無着色、やしゃ染め、顔料着色、染料着色

Actual Name: Toshikazu Shishido (b. 1960)
Place of Birth: Chiba Prefecture
Current Address: Saitama Prefecture
Began Carving Netsuke in: 1997
Former/Other Occupation(s): Precious-metal worker
Main Materials Used: Ivory, mammoth tusk, wood, amber
Favorite Subjects: Animals, plants, aquatic creatures
Main Types of Finish: Uncolored, *yasha* stain, paint, dyes

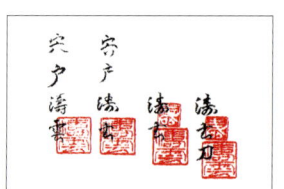

箱書き落款　Signature/seal on the box 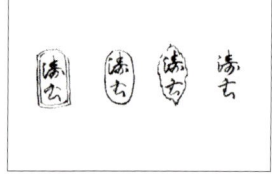　　銘　Signature

---

北村雲龍庵　UNRYUAN Kitamura

本名：北村辰夫（1952年生）
出身地：石川県輪島市
現住所：石川県輪島市
根付制作開始：1990年
根付制作以前／以外の仕事：漆器
主に使用している材料／材質：漆
得意とするテーマ：印籠に合わせた図案
主な仕上げ方：漆

Actual Name: Tatsuo Kitamura (b. 1960)
Place of Birth: Ishikawa Prefecture
Current Address: Ishikawa Prefecture
Began Carving Netsuke in: 1990
Former Occupation: Lacquer artist
Main Materials Used: Lacquer
Favorite Subjects: Coordinating *netsuke* and *inro* designs
Main Types of Finish: Lacquer

箱書き落款　Signature/seal on the box 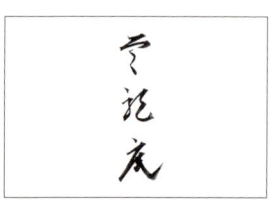　　銘　Signature

太田弥光　YAKO Ota

本名：太田量子（1947年生）
出身地：北海道
現住所：神奈川県横浜市
根付制作開始：1988年
根付制作以前／以外の仕事：美術工芸制作
主に使用している材料／材質：象牙、マンモス
　　牙、木材、鹿角
得意とするテーマ：動物、植物、魚
　　介類、鳥
主な仕上げ方：無着色、やしゃ染め、
　　顔料着色、染料着色、漆

Actual Name: Kazuko Ota (b. 1947)
Place of Birth: Hokkaido Prefecture
Current Address: Kanagawa Prefecture
Began Carving Netsuke in: 1988
Former/Other Occupation(s): Arts and crafts
Main Materials Used: Ivory, mammoth tusk, wood, stag antler
Favorite Subjects: Animals, plants, aquatic creatures, birds
Main Types of Finish: Uncolored, *yasha* stain, paint, dyes, lacquer

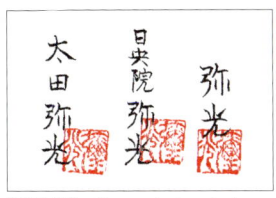

箱書き落款　Signature/seal on the box 　　　銘　Signature

斎藤保房　YASUFUSA Saito

本名：斎藤保雄（1931年生）
出身地：東京都
現住所：埼玉県比企郡
根付制作開始：1963年
根付制作以前／以外の仕事：象牙彫刻
主に使用している材料／材質：象牙、マンモス
　　牙、木材
得意とするテーマ：動物、植物
主な仕上げ方：無着色、やしゃ染め、
　　象嵌

Actual Name: Yasuo Saito (b. 1931)
Place of Birth: Tokyo
Current Address: Saitama Prefecture
Began Carving Netsuke in: 1963
Former/Other Occupation(s): Ivory carver
Main Materials Used: Ivory, mammoth tusk, wood
Favorite Subjects: Animals, plants
Main Types of Finish: Uncolored, *yasha* stain, inlay

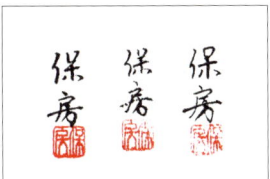

箱書き落款　Signature/seal on the box 　　　銘　Signature

山田洋治　YOJI Yamada

本名：山田洋治（1934年生）
出身地：大阪府
現住所：大阪府守口市
根付制作開始：1980年
主に使用している材料／材質：木材
得意とするテーマ：動物、妖怪、怪物
主な仕上げ方：無着色、やしゃ染め、染料着色

Actual Name: Yoji Yamada (b. 1934)
Place of Birth: Osaka Prefecture
Current Address: Osaka Prefecture
Began Carving Netsuke in: 1980
Main Materials Used: Wood
Favorite Subjects: Animals, imaginary beings
Main Types of Finish: Uncolored, *yasha* stain, dyes

箱書き落款　Signature/seal on the box 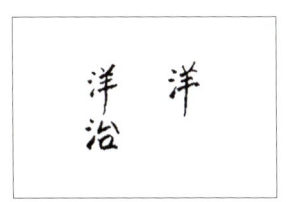　　　銘　Signature

向田陽佳　　YOKA Mukaida

本名：向田陽子（1968年生）
出身地：神奈川県
現住所：東京都大田区
根付制作開始：1998年
根付制作以前／以外の仕事：会社員
主に使用している材料／材質：象牙、マンモス
　　牙、木材、鹿角
得意とするテーマ：人物、動物
主な仕上げ方：無着色、やしゃ染め、
　　顔料着色

Actual Name: Yoko Mukaida (b. 1968)
Place of Birth: Kanagawa Prefecture
Current Address: Tokyo
Began Carving Netsuke in: 1998
Former/Other Occupation(s): Office worker
Main Materials Used: Ivory, mammoth tusk, wood, stag antler
Favorite Subjects: Human figures, animals
Main Types of Finish: Uncolored, *yasha* stain, paint

箱書き落款　Signature/seal on the box 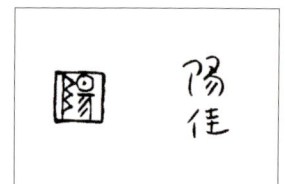　　　銘　Signature

阿部裕幸　　YUKO Abe

本名：阿部裕幸（1952年生）
出身地：群馬県
現住所：群馬県吾妻郡
根付制作開始：1992年
根付制作以前／以外の仕事：書家・篆刻家
主に使用している材料／材質：象牙
得意とするテーマ：動物、植物、魚介類、篆刻
　　と根付を融合させる篆刻根付
主な仕上げ方：無着色、やしゃ染め、
　　顔料着色、染料着色

Actual Name: Hiroyuki Abe (b. 1952)
Place of Birth: Gunma Prefecture
Current Address: Gunma Prefecture
Began Carving Netsuke in: 1992
Former/Other Occupation(s): Calligrapher, seal carver
Main Materials Used: Ivory
Favorite Subjects: Animals, plants, aquatic creatures, seal-type netsuke
Main Types of Finish: Uncolored, *yasha* stain, paint, dyes

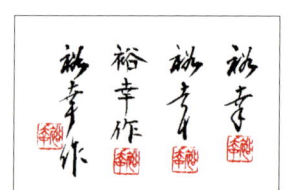

箱書き落款　Signature/seal on the box 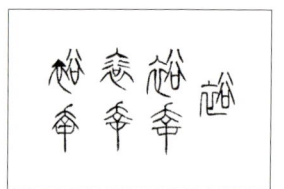　　　銘　Signature

小野里三昧　　ZANMAI Onosato

本名：小野里徹（1967年生）
出身地：東京都
現住所：東京都台東区
根付制作開始：1993年
根付制作以前／以外の仕事：古道具関係
主に使用している材料／材質：象牙、マンモス、
　　木材、鹿角
得意とするテーマ：動物
主な仕上げ方：無着色、やしゃ染め、
　　染料着色

Actual Name: Tetsu Onosato (b. 1967)
Place of Birth: Tokyo
Current Address: Tokyo
Began Carving Netsuke in: 1993
Former/Other Occupation(s): Antique business
Main Materials Used: Ivory, mammoth tusk, wood, stag antler
Favorite Subjects: Animals
Main Types of Finish: Uncolored, *yasha* stain, dyes

箱書き落款　Signature/seal on the box 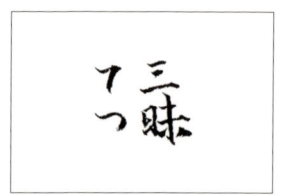　　　銘　Signature

マイケル・バーチ　Michael BIRCH

本名：マイケル・バーチ（1926年生）
出身地：英国
現住所：英国
根付制作開始：1973年
根付制作以前／以外の仕事：インダストリアル・デザイナー、光学・電気工学機器会社グループの創立、理事長・最高経営責任者、作家
主に使用している材料／材質：マンモス牙、木材（主に珍木材）、鹿角、海松、河馬の歯、琥珀
得意とするテーマ：特になし
主な仕上げ方：無着色、やしゃ染め、顔料着色、染料着色、漆、象嵌

Actual Name: Michael Henry Birch (b. 1926)
Place of Birth: United Kingdom
Current Address: United Kingdom
Began Carving Netsuke in: 1973
Former/Other Occupation(s): Industrial designer, CEO of a group of optics/electronics firms, writer
Main Materials Used: Mammoth tusk, wood (esp. exotic woods), stag antler, black coral, hippopotamus tooth, amber
Favorite Subjects: No preference
Main Types of Finish: Uncolored, *yasha* stain, paint, dyes, lacquer, inlay, etc.

銘　Signature

デーヴィッド・ブリッセット　David BLISSETT

本名：デーヴィッド・ブリッセット（1924年生）
出身地：英国
現住所：英国
根付制作開始：1971年
根付制作以前／以外の仕事：技師、治工具設計
主に使用している材料／材質：黄楊、象牙、河馬の歯、アフリカ・ブラックウッド、鹿角
得意とするテーマ：主に動物
主な仕上げ方：自然色、やしゃ染め、象嵌

Actual Name: David Blissett (b. 1924)
Place of Birth: United Kingdom
Current Address: United Kingdom
Began Carving Netsuke in: 1971
Former/Other Occupation(s): Engineer; tooling design
Main Materials Used: Boxwood, elephant ivory, hippopotamus tooth, African blackwood, stag antler
Favorite Subjects: Mainly animals
Main Types of Finish: Uncolored, *yasha* stain, inlay

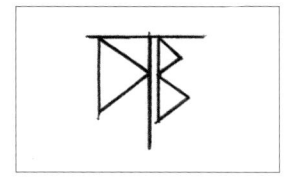

銘　Signature

ニック・ラム　Nick LAMB

本名：ニック・ラム（1948年生）
出身地：英国
現住所：アメリカ
根付制作開始：1983年
根付制作以前／以外の仕事：木彫
主に使用している材料／材質：木材（黄楊、黒檀、堅木）
得意とするテーマ：動物（霊長類）、鳥
主な仕上げ方：無着色、染料着色

Actual Name: Nicholas Kevin Lamb (b. 1948)
Place of Birth: United Kingdom
Current Address: United States
Began Carving Netsuke in: 1983
Former/Other Occupation(s): Wood sculptor
Main Materials Used: Wood (esp. boxwood, ebony, hardwoods)
Favorite Subjects: Animals (primates), birds
Main Types of Finish: Uncolored, dyes

銘　Signature

オーエン・マップ　Owen MAPP

本名：オーエン・マップ（1945年生）
出身地：ニュージーランド
現住所：ニュージーランド
根付制作開始：1969年
根付制作以前／以外の仕事：彫刻教師（美術学院等）
主に使用している材料／材質：象牙、化石化したセイウチ牙、鯨歯、骨材、石材（翡翠）
得意とするテーマ：ニュージーランドの自然と歴史
主な仕上げ方：無着色、染料着色

Actual Name: Owen Mapp (b. 1945)
Place of Birth: New Zealand
Current Address: New Zealand
Began Carving Netsuke in: 1969
Former/Other Occupation(s): Instructor of carving (New Zealand Academy of Fine Arts, etc)
Main Materials Used: Ivory, fossil walrus tusk, whale tooth, bone, stone (jade)
Favorite Subjects: New Zealand's nature and history
Main Types of Finish: Uncolored, dyes

銘　Signature

アーミン・ミュラー　Armin MÜLLER

本名：アーミン・ミュラー（1932年～2000年）
出身地：アメリカ
根付制作期間：1977年～2000年
根付制作以前／以外の仕事：窓ガラスの取り付け職人、陶芸家
主に使用している材料／材質：磁器（白磁と青磁の釉を用いた）
得意とするテーマ：自然、特に鳥、花、動物
主な仕上げ方：特になし

Actual Name: Armin Frederick Müller (1932-2000)
Place of Birth: United States
Carved Netsuke in: 1977-2000
Former/Other Occupation(s): Window glass installer, professional potter
Main Materials Used: Porcelain (with blanc-de-chine and celadon glazes)
Favorite Subjects: Nature, including birds, flowers, and animals
Main Types of Finish: None

銘　Signature

ガイ・ショー　Guy SHAW

本名：ガイ・ショー（1951年～2003年）
出身地：英国
根付制作期間：1978年～2003年
根付制作以前／以外の仕事：絵画、エッチング
主に使用している材料／材質：化石化したマンモスやセイウチ牙、鹿角、木材（流木も）、琥珀、骨材、石材
得意とするテーマ：葉、茸、魚、虫、種などを用いた自然
主な仕上げ方：やしゃ染め（時には過マンガン酸塩複合）、顔料着色（特にアクリル塗料）、染料着色、象嵌

Actual Name: Guy Shaw (1951-2003)
Place of Birth: United Kingdom
Carved Netsuke in: 1978-2003
Former/Other Occupation(s): Painting and etching
Main Materials Used: Fossilized mammoth and walrus tusk, stag antler, wood (also driftwood), bone, stone
Favorite Subjects: Nature, using leaves, fungi, fish, insects, and seeds
Main Types of Finish: *Yasha* stain, sometimes mixed with potassium permanganate, paint (esp. acrylics), dyes, inlay

銘　Signature

アンソニー・タウン　Anthony TOWNE

本名：アンソニー・タウン（1956年生）
出身地：アメリカ
現住所：アメリカ
根付制作開始：1990年
根付制作以前／以外の仕事：アメリカ森林局に勤務し、森林火災の消防と植樹に従事、オレゴン大学の非常勤講師
主に使用している材料／材質：胡桃
得意とするテーマ：仮面
主な仕上げ方：特になし、時々ナチュラル・オイル

Actual Name: Anthony Towne (b. 1956)
Place of Birth: United States
Current Address: United States
Began Carving Netsuke in: 1990
Former/Other Occupation(s): Worked for the U.S. Forestry Service, fighting fires and planting trees; taught as adjunct professor at the University of Oregon
Main Materials Used: Walnuts
Favorite Subjects: Masks
Main Types of Finish: No special finish, sometimes a little natural oil

銘　Signature

スーザン・レイト　Susan WRAIGHT

本名：スーザン・レイト（1956年生）
出身地：英国
現住所：オーストラリア
根付制作開始：1978年
根付制作以前／以外の仕事：ロンドンで宝石職人として訓練を受ける
主に使用している材料／材質：木材（多種多様な黄楊）：象嵌には琥珀、河馬の歯、螺鈿、金を用いる
得意とするテーマ：自然界を写し出す動物、特に蛙など小さくて一般に関心の薄い動物、イソップ物語
主な仕上げ方：無着色、染料着色

Actual Name: Susan Wraight (b. 1956)
Place of Birth: United Kingdom
Current Address: Australia
Began Carving Netsuke in: 1978
Former/Other Occupation(s): Trained as a jeweler in London
Main Materials Used: Wood (various types of boxwood); inlays include amber, hippopotamus tooth, mother-of-pearl, and gold
Favorite Subjects: Animals depicting the natural world, especially smaller and less considered ones like frogs, Aesop's fables
Main Types of Finish: Uncolored, dyes

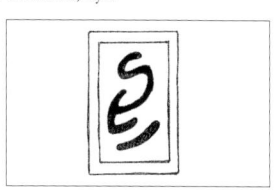

銘　Signature

根付　高円宮コレクションII	
定　　価	［本体4000円＋税］
発 行 日	2006年（平成18年）　1月11日　発行
編　　者	高円宮妃久子
デザイン	株式会社 トーヨー企画
発 行 所	株式会社 思文閣出版
	〒606−8203　京都市左京区田中関田町2−7
	電話 075−751−1781（代表）
印刷・製本	株式会社 図書同朋舎印刷
ISBN4-7842-1273-6 C1071	
協 力 者	赤井三夫／スティーヴン・コーミー／関戸健吾／
	ロベール・フレイシェル／牧野文蘭／山田英一／吉田ゆか里

© 2006 TAKAMADONOMIYAHI HISAKO

Printed in Japan

NETSUKE
The H.I.H. Prince Takamado Collection II

Price: 4,000yen+tax

Publication Date: January 11, 2006

Author: Her Imperial Highness Princess Takamado

Design: Toyo Kikaku Co., Ltd.

Publishing: Shibunkaku Publishing Co., Ltd.
　　　　　　2-7 Sekiden-cho, Tanaka
　　　　　　Sakyo-ku, Kyoto Japan
　　　　　　Phone: +81-75-751-1781

Printing: Tosho Insatsu Dohosha Co., Ltd.

ISBN4-7842-1273-6 C1071

Collaborators: Mitsuo Akai/Stephen Comee/Kengo Sekido/Robert Fleischel/
　　　　　　　　Wendy Makino/Hidekazu Yamada/Yukari Yoshida

All rights reserved. No part of this publication can be reproduced
in any form without the prior written permission of the publisher.